A CONSTITUTION

INFORMING THE FUTURE GUARDIANS OF LIBERTY

EVANGELIST CALEB GARRAWAY

Foreword by WWII Medal of Honor Recepient Hershel "Woody" Williams

America's Constitution

Copyright © 2011 Caleb & Katie Garraway

ISBN: 978-0-9832039-3-3

Faithful Life Publishers
3335 Galaxy Way
North Fort Myers, FL 33903
www.FaithfulLifePublishers.com
info@FLPublishers.com

EVANGELISM MINISTRIES
Caleb & Katie Garraway
5517 NW 23rd Street
Oklahoma City, OK 73127

www.thegarrawayfamily.com

Scripture quotations are from the Authorized King James Version

Printed in the United States of America

18 17 16 15 14 13 12 11   1 2 3 4 5

IF THE FOUNDATIONS BE DESTROYED,

what can the righteous do?

Evil will triumph...

IF GOOD MEN do nothing.

TABLE OF CONTENTS

FOREWORD

What an eye opener for all who call themselves Americans! A timely message at a time of peril. A writing that cries for every concerned American, all Christians and believers in creation, to seek the providence of God to save America. History has taught us that God keeps His promises: *"If my people, which are called by my name, shall humble themselves, and pray, and seek my face, and turn from their wicked ways; then will I hear from heaven, and will forgive their sin, and will heal their land" (II Chronicles 7:14).* Although we mortals do not know what the future holds, by seeking the providence of God, the Bible, and history, we can know who holds the future. I highly recommend that this book be read by every citizen, *especially the next generation,* and used in every Christian school of America.

Hershel "Woody" Williams
Marine Medal of Honor Recipient
Iwo Jima survivor by the grace of God our Creator

(Hershel Williams served as a United States Marine during World War II and participated in recapturing Guam and the invasion of Iwo Jima where he was wounded. Recommended by fellow Marines, he received the Medal of Honor, the nation's highest award for valor. In 1962, he became a Christian, began teaching Sunday School classes in 1963, and became a lay minister in 1965. He continues to be active in church, has held many committee chairmanships, and often speaks around the country. He has been apart of federal and state public service for 39 years and is Chaplain Emeritus of the Congressional Medal of Honor Society after serving as chaplain for 35 years.)

INTRODUCTION

At the beginning of time, God knew that one day a country of the West would rise and become one of the greatest nations in the history of the world. He knew that this nation would rise to prominence because it decided to base itself solidly upon the Word of God. This nation was the United States of America. Centuries have passed. Generations have come and gone. The Constitution has remained the same and has effectively guided us for over 235 years. However, we are currently facing a time in which liberals, revisionist historians, judicial activists, sodomites, and others are trying to secretly and slowly take away our liberties, our freedoms, our heritage, and our Biblical history. They are eagerly twisting the interpretation of our Constitution to suit their own agendas and fulfill their own demonic goals. Furthermore, liberals and judicial activists are trying to use the Constitution to purge all aspects of Christianity from the public square.

Throughout the centuries there has been a continual war raging between God and Satan – the principles from the Word of God against the philosophies emanating from the pit of Hell – the Spirit of God versus the spirit of the anti-Christ. This is the fight we are facing today in our government. The Bible says in I John 4:3, *"And every spirit that confesseth not that Jesus Christ is come in the flesh is not of God: and this is that spirit of antichrist, whereof ye have heard that it should come; and even now already is it in the world."* This spirit of anti-Christ has crept into our government over the past 60 years as we clearly see many trying to eradicate our freedoms and bring about unholy and ungodly legislation that goes directly against the principles of the Word of God and the Constitution itself. The battle is whether America is going to be a God-honoring nation – as it once was – or a godless nation.

Alexander Hamilton said, *"Those who stand for nothing fall for anything."* God is looking for a generation to arise who will realize that something is wrong with the current operation of our government as we seem to be doing "that which is right in our own eyes." God seeks a generation who will stand with the spirit of integrity *(morality backed with character)* and say, "Enough is enough!" This country is in desperate need of Christians, families, and young people who will arise to be part of the remnant to ensure the preservation of America on their watch. Thomas Jefferson warned us, *"All tyranny needs to gain a foothold is for people of good conscience to remain silent."* Will we remain silent or still? Or will we take advantage of the time in which we live and attempt to make a difference for the sake of future generations? We have every right to question any enemy - whether foreign or domestic – who will try to strip away our freedoms we hold dear. James Madison confirmed to us, *"We are **right** to take alarm at the first experiment upon our liberties."*

As long as we are alive in America, we should desire a God-honoring country! We are speaking of Jehovah God, the God of our Founding Fathers – not Allah or some other false deity. America was not a patchwork of religion, as President Barack Obama has mentioned, but a Judeo-Christian nation. John Adams said, *"The general principles upon which the fathers achieved independence are the general principles of Christianity."*

However, the world and most in Washington D.C. and in the news media do not accept this very plain truth. Therefore, we should be aware of the "alarm of war" resounding throughout our country as the liberal agenda is advancing, the sodomite agenda is advancing, the Communist agenda is advancing, the Muslim agenda is advancing, the satanic agenda of wickedness is advancing… Wake up, America! We must realize that we are at war, and if we want to preserve ourselves and desire our liberties to endure forever - we must stand and bring about a restoration back to the ways our founding fathers originally designed our country to be operated.

The liberal world is trying to take our liberties from us and rob us of our true heritage - to completely turn us away from the Bible — to <u>FULLY</u> <u>STRIP</u> us of who we are as a people.

The correct key to keep the light of liberty brightly burning can be found in the truth of Daniel Webster's statement: *"If we abide by the principles taught in the Bible, our country will go on prospering and to prosper; if we and our posterity shall be true to the Christian religion, if we and they shall live always in the fear of God and shall respect His commandments, we may have the highest hopes of the future fortunes of our country. But if we and our posterity neglect religious instruction and authority; violate the rules of eternal justice, trifle with the injunctions of morality, and recklessly destroy the political constitution which holds us together, no man can tell how sudden a catastrophe may overwhelm us and bury all our glory in profound obscurity."*

Our Founding Fathers KNEW that the Bible was the ONE and ONLY BOOK THAT WOULD GUIDE THIS NATION CORRECTLY… Under its principles LIBERTY would flourish… **THAT'S** why they STATED: *"We <u>hold</u> these truths to be self evident that all men…are <u>endowed</u> by their **Creator** with <u>certain</u> <u>unalienable</u> <u>rights</u>, among these are life, liberty, and the pursuit of happiness."*

On July 4, 1776, our founding fathers signed the Declaration of Independence, throwing off the tyranny of Great Britain and claiming their freedoms. Knowing they could not fight this great empire on their own but needed the mercies of Heaven to guide them, protect them, and help them, they implored the throne of God daily and begged for His power. And in the end, they were proudly able to stand victorious on the field of battle. As they faced the next task of creating their union, they knew the only way for them to survive and prosper as a nation was to base their newborn country upon the principles and precepts of God's Word. We will clearly find that they had dependency upon Almighty God!

We must know who we are as Americans. President Woodrow Wilson said, *"A nation which does not remember what it was yesterday, does not know what it is today. We are trying to do a futile thing if we do not know where we came from or what we have been about."* Therefore, it is important that the next generation is mindful what our Constitution is and how we received our liberties from the hand of God. George Washington said, *"A primary object…should be the education of our youth in the science of government. In a republic, what species of knowledge can be equally important? And what duty more pressing…than communicating it to those who are to be the future guardians of the liberties of the country?"* America's youth are the future guardians of our liberties. We must inform them of who we truly are as Americans. James Madison said, *"A well-instructed people alone can be permanently a free people."* If we desire to remain free, we must be well informed. The Bible says in Proverbs 28:2, *"by a man of understanding and knowledge the state thereof shall be prolonged."*

God has established three institutions among men: the family *(Genesis 2:22-25)*, the government *(Genesis 9:6)*, and the church *(Matthew 16:18)*. As Christians and as Americans, we have the responsibility and the opportunity to take care of God's institutions. According to our Constitution, "WE THE PEOPLE" are the government, and the representatives who sit in Washington, D.C. are our servants. In all reality, they are to serve the people, not themselves as they so often do. Therefore, we need to learn how our government works. We must be men and women of this knowledge, lest we be taken advantage of. We must understand its "politics" – the "science" or "policy" of the government. But, in order to understand the "science" of it, we must read and comprehend the "textbook" by which it is operated – the Constitution of the United States. The Constitution needs to be maintained, and we are to be the ones who will safeguard it from ravenous foes.

In I Timothy 6:20, God challenges us: *"Keep that which is committed to thy trust."* In I Corinthians 4:2, God says, *"Moreover it is required in stewards, that a man be found faithful."* A steward is one who takes care of his master's properties and possessions. God has given us the responsibility to "keep" his third institution – government. As His stewards, we must maintain it; we must preserve it in its original condition; we must keep it from being tampered with, misused, and ruined.

The way we can be good stewards of the government God has entrusted to us is to participate and have an active role in it. Being politically involved is a ministry. Three times in Romans 13:4-6, God refers to those who are politically active and are public servants (lawyer, police officer, etc.) as "ministers of God." He says, *"For he is the minister of God to thee for good. But if thou do that which is evil, be afraid; for he beareth not the sword in vain: for he is the minister of God, a revenger to execute wrath upon him that doeth evil. Wherefore ye must needs be subject, not only for wrath, but also for conscience sake. For for this cause pay ye tribute also: for they are God's ministers, attending continually upon this very thing."*

However, **before** we can become effective, active public servants and good stewards for God, **we must know the basic laws and liberties that are set forth in our Constitution.** Just like we need to read the instruction manual before putting something together, read the board game rules before we can correctly play, or read the codes of conduct before we can engage in an activity – we must read our Constitution to correctly understand the workings of our government so that we can effectively **be involved,** so that we can effectively **drive away those who wish to harm us and take advantage of us,** and so that we can effectively **instruct others in the truth of how it is to be operated.** It is our duty to *be informed,* to *be involved,* and to *be interceding (prayerfully and positionally)* for our country.

Charles Finney said, *"The time has come for Christians to vote for honest men…God cannot sustain this free and blessed country…unless the Church will take right ground. Christians must do their duty to their country as a part of their duty to God. It seems at times that the foundations of this Nation are rotten, and Christians seem to act as if they think God does not see what they do in politics. But I tell you, He does see, and He will bless or curse this nation according to the course Christians take in politics."* However, we cannot be involved and we cannot intercede if we are not first and foremost informed, unless we understand how unique we are as a people – called Americans.

This is vitally important…because if our government is not maintained, it will continue to grow. If it grows without the Constitutional guidance of its people, it will begin to reel out of control. Thomas Jefferson said that the government should be symbolized as "the beast" that needs to be restrained so that it does not inflict "cruel and unusual punishment" upon its citizens. He said, *"The two enemies of the people are criminals and government, so let us tie the second down with the chains of the Constitution so the second will not become the legalized version of the first."* We have not heeded these words; we have turned our back on our government, and it has become untamed animal - doing as it pleases. We have increased inappropriate and unbearable taxation upon the masses, we have torturously murdered over 53 million unborn American citizens, and we have proceeded to interpret the Constitution to meet our own needs. The Constitution is <u>NOT</u> *"the most marvelously elastic compilation of rules of government ever written"* as President Franklin Delano Roosevelt incorrectly stated; it is a chain - a chain with which we must shackle up "the beast" to keep it from unnecessarily harming the populace. Patrick Henry declared that *"[t]he Constitution is <u>not</u> an instrument for the government to restrain the people, it is an instrument for the people to restrain the government."*

Through our studies in ***America's Constitution: Informing the Future Guardians of Liberties***, we want to grow aware of our American Christian heritage, to glimpse the history behind the writing of the Constitution, and to understand how our government is to be operated by this very sacred document. We desire to see how God, His Word, and His men were thoroughly involved in founding of our nation and how we as Christians can remain faithful to our God, our country, and our Constitution.

So with this in mind, let us take a look into our precious past… let us step back into time to the mid-1700's just prior to the War for Independence and observe how this great nation was born and how our Constitution was formed. Let us examine, in brief, how we became the United States of America - *"one nation **under God**, indivisible, with liberty and justice for all."*

Chapter I

Rejection of Tyranny
The Events Leading to the War for Independence

In the early days of our history, the colonists were experiencing tyranny from Great Britain – they realized that they were not truly walking with liberty. Knowing they could not fight this great empire on their own but needed the mercies of Heaven to guide them, protect them, and help them, they implored the throne of God daily and begged for His power. And in the end, they were proudly able to stand victorious on the field of battle. Our Founding Fathers were **men**, settled in their character, reputation, and principles. Many could have lived lives of ease had they been willing to follow the dictatorial whims of the King of Britain. But they refused to be puppets, to be stepped upon, to be drained of their finances through extensive and unconstitutional taxation without proper representation in the English Parliament. They determined that they had only one true King – His name was King Jesus. Committees began to meet and a Continental Congress was formed. There was turmoil about whether or not they should stand and literally fight against the vast empire of England, but one man stood in their midst with undaunted courage and summarized the colonial spirit by proclaiming, *"...We must fight! I repeat it, we must fight! An appeal to arms and to the God of Hosts is all that is left us! ...We are not weak, if we make a proper use of the means which the God of nature hath placed in our power. Three millions of people, armed in the Holy causes of liberty, and in such a country as that which we possess, are invincible* *by any force which our enemy can send against us. Besides, we shall not fight our battle alone. There is a just God who presides over the destinies of nations, and who will raise up friends to fight our battle for us. The battle…is not to the strong alone; it is to the vigilant, the active, the brave….* **Is life so dear or peace so sweet as to be purchased at the price of chains and slavery? Forbid it, Almighty God! I know not what course others may take; but as for me, give me liberty or give me death!***"* This man was the notable fiery orator Patrick Henry.

In 1763 the French and Indian Wars, a series of conflicts between Great Britain and France on American soil in which many of the signers of the Declaration of Independence and their ancestors fought, ended in treaty.

King George III – young, idealistic, and inexperienced, becoming king of the world's greatest empire by the age of 22 toward the end of the French and Indian War – thought it wise to begin taxing the American colonies to replenish the British treasury for all the expenses it incurred during the French and Indian War. Since the War was fought on American soil concerning American territory, it only seemed fitting for the colonies to pay more to reduce those debts and to support the cost of administering the newly acquired territories in North America. The King's strength was his stubbornness, seldomly admitting to his mistakes or yielding to anyone else's opinions, and his mind was set to tax. In 1765, the passing of the "Stamp Act" – requiring tax to be paid on all printed papers, from official documents to playing cards – infuriated many colonists. Our forefathers saw themselves as an extension of the territory and land of Great Britain. In order to be properly and appropriately taxed by the British government, the Colonies, they believed, should have had delegates representing them; but the Parliament and King George III would have none of that, instead taxing them without representation. Therefore, nine of the thirteen colonies banded together to limit the importation of British goods. Defiantly, Parliament quickly passed the "Declaratory Act," proclaiming that they had every right to make future laws governing and taxing the colonies no matter how the Colonies may resist in disapproval. The King was oblivious of the essential, vital bond shared between the British Empire and the American Colonies…his only major concern was his obsession with obedience to the Crown.

On May 15, 1767, Parliament passed the infamous "Townshend Acts," which levied taxes on all the widely used products throughout the Colonies – glass, lead, pain, paper, and tea – and instituted a new bureaucracy in America to enforce the collection of taxes, to limit boycotting, and to catch any smugglers and their "contraband."

Things only got worse as the years went on. King George III, the Prime Minister's cabinet, and most of Parliament had the focused mindset of bringing "the rebels" to their knees…to make them pay for their disloyalty. In March, 1774, British Parliament passed several laws which they called the Coercive Acts. The colonists referred to them as the "Intolerable Acts." Among others, these included the "Boston Port Act," which closed the port of Boston, and the "Quartering Act," which demanded colonists house British soldiers whenever deemed necessary.

"We have no King but Jesus!" became the colonies' rallying cry for American independence from the unlawful tyranny of England. In 1774, the Massachusetts Congress issued the formal declaration, *"Resistance to tyranny becomes the Christian and social duty of each individual… Continue steadfast, and with a proper sense of your dependence on God, nobly defend those rights which heaven gave, and no man ought to take from us."*

In September, 1774, the first Continental Congress convened. Later that year, the Articles of Association were signed, in which the colonies agree to a nonimportation, no consumption, and nonexportation stance with the British.

On September 6, 1774, word spread that the British were going to cannonade Boston. Prayer was held in the Continental Congress the following morning by Pastor Jacob Duche, along with the reading and mediating upon Psalm 35. John Adams relates in a letter to his wife, Abigail, *"I never saw a greater effect upon an audience. It seem as if heaven had ordained that Psalm to be read on that morning. After this, Mr. Duche, unexpectedly to every body, struck out into an extemporary prayer, which filled the bosom of every man present. I must confess, I never heard a better prayer, or one so well pronounced."*

Colonists began to form militias, organizing themselves to protect their communities from the British. They were generally laymen from a particular local church and were led by their pastor or a deacon who normally conducted military drills after Sunday services. However, those who were able to assemble at a moment's notice were called the Minutemen. In 1774, the Congress of Massachusetts recognized their significance and challenged them, *"The eyes not only of North America and the whole British Empire, but of all Europe, are upon you. Let us be, therefore, altogether solicitous that no disorderly behavior, nothing unbecoming our characters as Americans, as citizens and Christians, be justly chargeable to us."*

The colonists at Lexington and Concord were the first to earn this noble name of MINUTEMEN. Pastor Jonas Clark in Lexington continually warned his congregation and the people of that peaceful community that one day the British would come and destroy their homes if they would not stand and defend what was given to them by God. When the British came – they were ready.

On April 18, 1775, British General Thomas Gage sent 700 soldiers to destroy guns and ammunition the colonists had stored in the town of Concord, just outside of Boston. They also planned to secretly arrest Samuel Adams and John Hancock while they were in Lexington. Since John Hancock's cousin was the wife of Pastor Jonas Clark, oftentimes, these two men would meet with other colonial delegates in the home of Pastor Clark to discuss the points of liberty and the appropriate plans for action against the tyranny of Great Britain.

Dr. Joseph Warren, a Massachusetts physician in charge of the Boston's militia, learned of these British plans and sent Paul Revere to spread the warning.

Just in case he would not be able to get out of Boston with the message, Revere planned to alert the people and other riders by using lanterns in the Old North Church steeple as a signal...one lantern if the British were coming by land, and two lanterns if the British were coming by sea.

On the evening of April 18th, the British troops ferried quietly across the Boston Harbor to start their march on Lexington. Revere hung both lanterns in the church steeple. Then he, William Dawes, and Dr. Samuel Prescott began their legendary midnight ride under the pale moonlight to warn the citizens of Lexington and Concord and to alert their fellow patriots, John Hancock and Samuel Adams, that the British were coming.

In the early dawn of April 19th, when the British soldiers reached Lexington, both of the colonial leaders had escaped. Captain Jonas Parker and 75 armed Minutemen were stationed in the town square – prepared to meet the British, though they would be greatly outnumbered. Captain John Parker ordered his men to not *"fire unless fired upon, but if they want a war let it begin here."* The British delivered their first volley of musket balls, American patriots bravely fought to protect their homes and their God-given rights of life, liberty, and the pursuit of happiness. Eight Minutemen died that day under the shadow of their church's steeple. One had been slain when a stray British bullet caught him and killed him as he was about to go through the doorway of the church to gather more gunpowder that was being stored there. Another ten colonists were injured during the fight.

Pastor Jonas Clark declared after the battle, reflecting on the barbarism of the British, *"And this is the place where the fatal scene begins! They approach with the morning light; and more like murderers and cutthroats, than the troops of a Christian king, without provocation, without warning, when no war was proclaimed, they draw the sword of violence, upon the inhabitants of this town, and with the cruelty and barbarity, which would have made the most hardened savage blush, they shed INNOCENT BLOOD…. Yonder field can witness the innocent blood of our brethren slain! There the tender father bled, and there the beloved son!"* He concluded by solemnly stating: *"From this day,"* as he gazed upon the dead bodies of the men from his congregation, *"will be dated the liberty of the world."* And of a truth, this battle began the birth of American freedom.

Although Paul Revere was captured by British scouts before reaching Concord, other messengers managed to get through and warn the people. While the British soldiers continued on their way to Concord, the men and women of Concord were busy moving the arms and ammunition to new hiding places in surrounding towns. When the soldiers arrived, they were only able to destroy part of the supplies.

The War for Independence had begun.

Less than two months after the battles at Lexington and Concord, on June 12, 1775, Congress issued a call for all citizens to fast, pray, and confess their sins that God might bless the land as they began to battle against the mightiest of empires. *"And it is recommended to Christians, of all denominations, to assemble for public worship, and to abstain from servile labour and recreations on said day."*

Interestingly, after the War for Independence, when one notable British general was asked what he had feared the most during the conflict, he replied that it was not General Washington, the Continental Army, the French navy, the diverse terrain, or even the weather - but the Minutemen: *"Those crazy soldiers were improperly armed and barely clothed, but the American Minutemen did not know the meaning of the word 'retreat.' If you ever wanted to gain a victory over the Minutemen, you had to kill them all because they never quit."* This should remain the testimony of ALL Americans who will still stand for freedom and Biblical faith in America.

CHAPTER II

DIVINE INTERVENTION
The Hand of God in the Fight for Freedom

There were many instances during the War for Independence when God providentially guided our fledgling nation at precise moments, worked in their behalf through supernatural circumstances, and protected them from grave danger. When the American colonists rose victorious over the British Empire in 1781, it was more than just a "coincidence" – more than just a string of good luck and fortunate occurrences. Something or *Someone* other than human skill and ingenuity *was* at work to have orchestrated the safekeeping of our Founding Fathers and the extraordinary sequence of military engagements that led to the colonies' glorious victory. General George Washington said, *"If I should be able to rise superior to these and many of the other difficulties…I shall most religiously believe that the finger of Providence is in it, to blind the eyes of our enemies."* Consider a handful of marvelous moments when God directly protected and guided our newborn nation in conflict.

THE PRESERVATION OF GEORGE WASHINGTON

By all accounts, George Washington should have been killed in the French and Indian War, but was miraculously (not mysteriously) protected. At the Battle at the Monongahela, Washington and the British army were ambushed by the French and Indians. Every officer on horseback was killed except for Washington. He later wrote to his brother John on July 18, 1755:

"But by the all-powerful dispensations of Providence, I have been protected beyond all human probability or expectation; for I had four bullets through my coat, and two horses shot under me, yet escaped unhurt, although death was leveling my companions on every side of me."

Washington was only 23 when he eluded the cold grasp of death on the battlefield. He emerged unscathed with his faith deeper and stronger than ever. God had protected him, and unknown to Washington, God had a great purpose for his life – to become the Commander-in-Chief of the greatest war for independence ever fought in the history of mankind. When he received this position, in a letter to his wife he explained, *"I shall rely confidently on that Providence which has heretofore preserved and been bountiful to me."* He thoroughly understood that God had preserved him for this very purpose.

During the years of the War for Independence, Washington would continually move about the battlefield among the troops with little regard for his own personal safety – showing his resolve and the importance of being involved. In September, 1777, at Germantown, Pennsylvania, however, Washington should have died but yet was somehow preserved – again. The British were advancing on Philadelphia; the Colonial Army was attempting to cut them off, and both armies were coming relatively close to each other along the banks of the Brandywine River. On September 7, British Captain Patrick Ferguson with three of his men was scouting ahead for the British near Chadd's Ford. They soon came upon two American officers on horseback just a short distance away from their position. Ferguson and his men swiftly raised their rifles to ambush them, but the officers suddenly turned away and soon there was too much distance between the two parties for the British to quickly shoot them down. Captain Ferguson later accounted, *"It was not pleasant to fire at the back of an unoffending individual who was acquitting himself coolly of his duty, and so I let him alone."* Later, Ferguson learned that the man he had preserved was General Washington.

After every victory, Washington gave credit for their survival and success to Almighty God. After the victory of Yorktown, which marked the end of the War for Independence, he ordered preaching services to be held throughout the army to express the *"gratitude of heart which the recognition of such reiterated and astonishing interpositions of Providence demand of us."*

THE BATTLE OF BUNKER HILL

After the battles at Lexington and Concord, the British troops retreated back to Boston and concentrated their forces in that area. Most of the local militias from Massachusetts and nearby colonies agreed to join together loosely under the command of General Ward until Congress had commissioned Washington as the commander-in-chief.

Meanwhile, among the British ranks, Admiral Samuel Graves strongly suggested to Commander-in-Chief General Thomas Gage that they needed to secure the high ground in the proximity of Boston and Charlestown to protect their fleet. Gage dismissed this idea, however, and thought it better to pull all of his troops onto the Boston peninsula. The colonists discovered this plan and decided to make a daring move to occupy the high ground that the British had so foolishly surrendered.

Unknown to the British, on the dusk of June 16, 1775, Colonel William Prescott with his 800+ men quietly and quickly crossed the Charlestown Neck and set up camp on Breed's Hill. With picks and shovels they constructed a redoubt about six feet high on the hillside. Colonel John Stark and his men joined these forces and decided to position themselves to the north along a rail fence, building a stone wall behind it for extra protection. This position was easily open for British naval gunfire. However, since no one had taken the time during the British occupation to chart these waters, Admiral Graves refused to risk one of his vessels to go through them in order to attack the Americans. From Boston Harbor, the British would have quickly prevailed, and the colonists would have been slaughtered. Yet the providence of God was guiding their every step, and now the high ground was occupied by 1,500 American minutemen.

At dawn of the following morning, crewmen on the *HMS Lively* noticed this amazing American activity and immediately sounded the alarm. General Gage held a council of war. Blinded with pride, he soon erected a battle plan of massive assault directly up the hill and placed General Howe in command of the operation.

The British were about to advance on the fortified positions. The Americans placed stakes about forty yards in front of their embankments and ordered no one to open fire until the British had reached that stake. Exhausted, hungry, and thirsty, men readied themselves and their muskets for this major conflict. As the fighting was soon to commence, one unknown officer proclaimed to his uneasy troops, *"Don't one of you fire until you see the white of their eyes!"*

The British brought a number of cannons from their warships out in Boston harbor to decimate the American fortifications. Once positioned, they opened with a flurry of thunder and fire…but within a few minutes the sounds of the guns mysteriously ceased. Confused, Howe demanded to know what was going on. Soon, he received word that someone had packed the wrong sized cannon balls in the side boxes…and that none of the artillery would be able to reach the high ground. The 200+ naval guns of the British warships out in Boston Harbor also attempted to blast away the colonists, but the cannonballs aimed at Bunker Hill and Breed's Hill either passed over the top of the redoubt or harmlessly impacted the hillside.

The first and second waves of British regiments were devastated with overwhelming volleys. However, as the third wave approached, they began to push back the American forces, since the colonists had exhausted a large quantity of their ammunition. Though the Continental Army did not win the battle, they did not suffer nearly as much causality as the British, and achieved a moral victory by showing the world that they could successfully repel the strongest of British waves.

BOSTON & DORCHESTER HEIGHTS

After the Battle of Bunker Hill, the British failed to pursue the "rebels" as they withdrew from the Boston peninsula. As the loosely formed Continental Army regathered forces, on July 6, 1775, Congress passed "The Declaration of the Causes and Necessity of Taking Up

Arms," urging colonists to join in the fight. Congress concluded by stating: *"With a humble confidence in the mercies of the Supreme and impartial God and ruler of the universe, we most devoutly implore His divine goodness to protect us happily through this great conflict,..."*

When the newly appointed Commander-in-Chief George Washington arrived shortly thereafter, this unknown favor from the British granted him precious time and space to tackle a formidable challenge before him – assembling the Continental Army into a fighting force ready to combat the world's mightiest military. Tirelessly he worked – enlisting, organizing, and training numerous militias to become a uniform body. Washington reported to Congress, *"It is not in the pages of history, perhaps, to furnish a case like ours. To maintain a post within musket-shot of the enemy, for six months together, without powder, and at the same time to disband one army, and recruit another, within that distance of twenty-odd British regiments, is more, probably, than ever was attempted. But if we succeed...I shall think it the most fortunate event of my whole life."* British General Howe received word during this time that Washington and the Continental Army were in a turmoil with little powder or ammunition, but he chose not to believe it and continued to hold his forces back in the comforts of Boston. Truly, the colonists were able to succeed by the protective hand of God. This accomplishment became one of the greatest yet least recognized feats of military history.

The British were satisfied with just defending Boston and ensuring its fortifications. Only British General Clinton, irritated with the English apathy of not continuing to pursue the enemy, strongly urged General Howe to consider taking Dorchester Heights, high ground across the Boston Harbor that was unoccupied by either side. Howe dismissed this advice, reasoning that since the Americans did not have major artillery, there would be no need to waste troops there. However, for precautionary purposes, a task force was formed about a week after the Battle of Bunker Hill, but the operation was continually postponed for over seven months – until they woke up on March 5, 1776, and realized it was too late. The British were wrong about the American ingenuity and decisiveness.

Colonel Benedict Arnold, Ethan Allen, and their Green Mountain Boys captured the British stronghold, Fort Ticonderoga, on May 9, 1775, by surprise with few shots fired. Ethan Allen beat on the door of Captain William Delaplace to wake him out of sleep and force him to surrender his forces. Stalling for time, Captain Delaplace's lieutenant requested to know what right they had to make such demands. Ethan Allen boldly proclaimed, *"In the name of the Great Jehovah and the Continental Congress."* The Continental Army captured a large number of cannons and firearms, kegs of gunpowder, and barrels of ammunition. Henry Knox, a close friend of General Washington's, went to Fort Ticonderoga and brought this arsenal back during the winter of 1775 – moving sixty tons of munitions over three hundred miles. Unknown to General Howe, they arrived to Washington's position near Boston, Massachusetts, in late January, 1776. By early February, over 17,000 men had joined the Continental Army. Because of this great advantage, Washington and his men decided to make their attack on March 4, 1776, from Dorchester Heights – the opportune high ground which the British had ignored.

On the evening of March 2, Washington ordered the Army's new cannons to begin bombarding the British from Roxbury Hill to engage their attention, occupy their time in returning fire, and distract them from the colonists' primary plans. The sound of cannon fire and clouds of smoke greatly helped disguise the Continental Army's advance upon Dorchester Heights during the night of March 4. Providentially, the wind blew from the southwest, carrying sound away from Boston and causing the smoke of the colonists' Roxbury batteries to drift across the harbor, adding to the thick haze that already hung over Boston.

As the Continental Army was on the move and setting up fortifications, a British officer received word around 10:00 PM that *"the rebels were at work on Dorchester Heights."* He, in turn, reported this to Brigadier General Francis Smith, who was not famous for his initiative. Lazily, he did nothing with this information and did not take any action to confirm it. None of the British cannons fired upon Dorchester Heights that night, and no one prepared troops or made any plans. The British woke up the following morning to find the Americans once again occupying the high ground – a deja vu of the Battle of Bunker Hill.

General Howe stared at this sight and remarked, *"The rebels have done more in one night than my whole army would have done in months."* He ordered his cannons to fire upon the colonist fortifications, but neither the shore batteries nor the warships in Boston harbor could elevate their guns high enough to reach the Continental Army.

The British quickly loaded men and supplies into vessels to ferry across the harbor, land on the beaches of Dorchester Heights, and begin their bold uphill attack. At this point though, the weather took an unexpected turn. A sudden storm arose and made the British crossing impossible, scattering their vessels about the harbor and driving some aground. It was reported as a "hurricane" and was of an intensity that few had ever experienced. The storm continued through the night until the next morning. Fearing that the colonists had strengthened their positions even more, the British withdrew their forces back into the Boston garrison, and General Howe ordered an evacuation. This is what General Washington inwardly hoped would occur, and God graciously answered his prayer. Since the British had limited space on their vessels, they left a considerable amount of munitions, weapons (including over 200 cannons), and horses behind for the colonists to claim and add to their supplies.

This amazing victory was no accident, but all orchestrated in God's plan for America. Instead of a celebration praising their own military accomplishments, Washington requested for his men to attend church services with grateful hearts filled with thanksgiving. These events caused our nation to surge forward toward declaring our independence and throwing off the tyranny of Great Britain.

SIGNING OF THE DECLARATION OF INDEPENDENCE

The American colonists tried very hard during the 1760's and 1770's to avoid war with the British Empire; but King George III's and Parliament's arrogance and obsession to control colonial commerce, combined with the colonists' fear that the Church of England would be soon imposed over them as a state church – America was compelled to claim their independence.

By early 1776, Congress received word back from Great Britain that their Olive Branch Petition was rejected by the King. He declared that the colonies were in *"open and avowed rebellion"* and that the British Empire would *"use their utmost endeavours to withstand and suppress such rebellion…"* and that *"blows must decide whether they are to be subject to this country or to be independent."* The delegates were in a turmoil – at an impasse – not sure whether or not to go through with the declaration of their independence or still try to work it out with the British. However, when Congress received word on March 23, 1776, that the Continental Army had forced the British to retreat and abandon Boston, their mindset and the tone of their debates changed. On June 7, 1776, Richard Henry Lee stood among his fellow representatives and urged them to recognize *"that these United Colonies are, and of a right ought to be, free and independent states."* In full agreement, they pressed forward with the formulation of the Declaration of Independence. John Adams said, *"It is the will of heaven that the two countries should be sundered forever."* Our founding fathers recognized clearly now that true independence was only achieved by obedience to God through rebellion against unbiblical tyranny.

After listing their 27 grievances and explaining the tyrannical acts of King George III, our Founding Fathers publicly yet humbly called upon God to rightly discern between the actions of the British Empire and the fledgling American colonies. All of the world could read the testimony and request toward the end of this sacred document, *"We, therefore, the Representatives of the united States of America, in General Congress, Assembled, appealing to the Supreme Judge of the world for the rectitude of our intentions, do, in the Name, and by Authority of the good People of these Colonies, solemnly publish and declare, That these United Colonies are, and of Right ought to be Free and Independent States; that they are Absolved from all Allegiance to the British Crown, and that all political connection between them and the State of Great Britain, is and ought to be totally dissolved;…"* Our Founding Fathers asked God to judge this case on the Eternal scale, evaluating the prosecution and tyranny of Great Britain and the defense and motive of the American Colonies, and to favor the side of the right. This was no longer about who had the bigger army, the more firepower, or the best policies. American colonists put their fate in the hand of God and pleaded for His providential protection, as they believed they were completing a necessary, Biblical task.

Our founding fathers were not "wild-eyed, rabble-rousing ruffians." They were stately men of character and education. Eighteen of the signers were merchants, fourteen were farmers, and four were doctors. Twenty-two were lawyers, and nine were judges. Stephen Hopkins had been governor of Rhode Island. Forty-two signers had served in the colonial legislatures. Nine of the signers were immigrants, two were brothers, and two were cousins. One was an orphan. The average age of the delegates was 45. Benjamin Franklin was the oldest at 70, and Thomas Lynch Jr. was the youngest at 27. They were diverse, but they all equally valued liberty – more than anything else. Standing tall together, unwaveringly, they pledged at the end of the Declaration of Independence, *"For the pledge of this declaration, with a firm reliance on the protection of the Divine Providence, we mutually pledge to each other, our lives, our fortunes, and our sacred honor."* Samuel Adams rejoiced, exclaiming, *"We have this day restored the Sovereign to Whom all men ought to be obedient. He reigns in heaven and from the rising to the setting of the sun, let His kingdom come."* Benjamin Franklin somberly reminded his fellow delegates at the signing of the Declaration of Independence, *"We must all hang together, gentlemen, or else we shall most assuredly hang separately."*

Many of these men fought in the war effort. Among these were William Whipple and Oliver Wolcott. Whipple served with the New Hampshire militia and was a commanding officer in the decisive Saratoga victory. Wolcott led the Connecticut regiments sent for the defense of New York and commanded a brigade of militia that took part in the defeat of General Burgoyne.

They certainly suffered for their stand. Five of the signers were captured by the British as traitors, and tortured before they died. Twelve of them had their homes ransacked and burned. Two lost their sons while fighting in the Continental Army and another had two sons captured. Nine others fought and died from wounds or hardships they experienced as they gave their last full measure for our freedoms.

Specifically, Carter Baxton of Virginia, a wealthy planter and trader, watched his own ships destroyed by the British Navy. He sold his home and all his properties to pay off his debts and he died in poverty. Thomas McKeam served in the Continental Congress voluntarily without pay, even after all his possessions were taken from him by the British. He once wrote to John Adams that he was being "hunted like a fox" by the enemy, compelled to move his family more than five times in just a few months from hiding place to hiding place. The British and the loyalists plundered the properties and homes of Congressmen Ellery, Clymer, Hall, Walton, Gwinnett, Heyward, Ruttledge, and Middleton. Francis Lewis and his family fled as the British came and destroyed their home. However, his wife was captured and thrown into jail. Lewis was unable to successfully locate her and rescue her before she died a few months later. John Hart was driven from the bedside of his wife as she lay dying with sickness. His fields and his grist mill had already been laid to waste by previous British raids. He had sent out all thirteen of his children to flee for their lives before the British surprised them again and it was too late for them all. For more than a year he lived in the forests and caves, on the run to evade capture. After the War for Independence, he returned to the ruins of his house to find his wife had died and his children were gone, no where to be found. At the Battle of Yorktown at the end of the War, Thomas Nelson, Jr., noticed that British General Cornwallis had taken his home to become the British headquarters. Nelson quietly urged General Washington to open fire upon his own property, regardless of the damage that would be done. The war was won, but the properties were destroyed and Nelson died bankrupt. On July 4, 1776, each of these men had stood proudly, excitedly, and undauntedly...ready to face what their fates might be. The price of liberty to them was *priceless*.

On July 2, Congress approved the wording for the Declaration of Independence. On July 4, the delegates voted to accept it. John Adams wrote, *"I am apt to believe that it will be celebrated by succeeding generations as the great anniversary Festival. It ought to be commemorated, as the Day of Deliverance, by solemn acts of devotion to God Almighty. It ought to be solemnized with pomp and parade, with shows, games, sports, guns, bells, bonfires, and illuminations, from one end of this continent to the other, from this time forward forever."*

In America's "birth certificate" – the Declaration of Independence – God is referenced four times specifically. Consider the following excerpts:

- *"The Laws of Nature and of Nature's God"* – referring to God's natural laws for the Universe understood through science and God's will revealed in the Bible
- *"All Men are created equal, they are endowed by their Creator with certain unalienable Rights"* – referring to God the Creator in the book of Genesis chapter one
- *"Appealing to the Supreme Judge of the World for the Rectitude of our Intentions"* – referring to God as the One Who judges and evaluates all things in His righteousness
- *"With a firm Reliance on the Protection of Divine Providence"* – referring to God Who will lovingly guide His people in the midst of perilous times

Very importantly, a key statement made in the Declaration of Independence is: *"We hold these truths to be self-evident, that all men are created equal, that they are endowed by their Creator with certain unalienable Rights, that among these are Life, Liberty, and the pursuit of Happiness. – That to secure these rights, Governments are instituted among Men,…"* Our Founding Fathers believed that there were a few things about government and men's rights that were plain and simple. First, all men are the same in the sight of God – we have the same nature and are created in His image. Therefore, we have a duty to keep and to respect this in both ourselves and others. This duty naturally demands certain rights – the right to resist an effort to dishonor or violate the image of God in us. Therefore, GOD is the source of our freedoms…NOT the government. The government has simply been instituted to secure and protect these God-given rights that we hold dear – NOT grant them to us or deny them from us.

Thomas Jefferson was the penman of the Declaration of Independence. An interesting note is that Thomas Jefferson was influenced by the independent Baptists of his time and by the writings of Roger Williams, the founder of Rhode Island. Thomas Armitage, in his book *History of the Baptists,* accounts that *"there was a small Baptist church which held its monthly meetings for business at a short distance from Mr. Jefferson's house. Mr. Jefferson attended these meetings for several months in succession. The pastor on one occasion asked him how he was pleased with their church government. Mr. Jefferson replied that it struck him with great force and had interested him much, that he considered it the only form of true democracy then existing in the world, and had concluded that it would be the best plan of government for the American colonies."* This was about eight to ten years before he wrote the Declaration of Independence and before the War for Independence. Jefferson greatly admired the zeal and courage of Bible-believing Baptists and envisioned a republic styled after the order of their church.

Thomas Jefferson mentioned in his writings that when he penned the Declaration of Independence, the principles within the document were not original to him, but were instead, *"intended to be an expression of the American mind."* Many historians believe that Jefferson received these ideas and principles from the writings of John Locke; however, forty-five years *before* Locke began his writings, the widely-read American Baptist preacher, Roger Williams, wrote the exact concepts that we find in our Declaration of Independence. Interestingly, *both* men – John Locke and Roger Williams – were heavily influenced by the writings of an *anonymous Baptist minister* who was wrongly imprisoned at the Newgate prison in England back in 1620. This preacher wrote his "tract," which he called *"Humble Supplication,"* upon parchment with milk, so it could only be read if it was burnt with candles.

Notice the similarities between the thoughts of Pastor Williams and the principles of liberty in the Declaration of Independence:

- First, whereas they say, that the Civill order may erect and establish what forme of civill Government may seem in wisedome most meet, I acknowledge the proposition to be most true, both in itself, and also considered with the end of it, that **a civill Government is an Ordinance of God, to conserve the civill peace of people**, so farre as concerns their Bodies and Goods, as formerly hath beene said.

- But from the Grant I infer, that the Soveraigne, originall, and **foundation of civill power lies in the people**, (whom they must needs meane by the civill power distinct from the Government set up.) And if so, that **a People may erect and establish what forme of Government seemes to them most meete for their civill condition: It is evident that such Governments as are by them erected and established, have no more power, nor for no longer time, then the civill power or people consenting and agreeing shall betrust them with.** *This is **cleere** not only in **Reason**, but in the experience of all common-weales, where the people are not deprived of their naturall freedome by the power of the Tyrants* (Roger Williams, *The Complete Writings of Roger Williams, Vol. 3, The Bloudy Tenet of Persecution,* p. 249-250).

- We hold these truths to be **self-evident**, that all men are created equal, that they are endowed by their Creator with certain unalienable Rights, that among these are Life, Liberty and the pursuit of Happiness. – That **to secure these rights, Governments are instituted among Men, deriving their just powers from the consent of the governed**, – That whenever any Form of Government becomes destructive of these ends, **it is the Right of the People to alter or to abolish it, and to institute new Government, laying its foundation on such principles and organizing its powers in such form, as to them shall seem most likely to effect their Safety and Happiness** (Thomas Jefferson, *The Declaration of Independence*).

On July 8, the Declaration was publicly read for the first time on the steps of Independence Hall, accompanied by the ringing of the Liberty Bell. (As a side note, the "cracked" Liberty Bell of Independence Hall in Philadelphia was originally made in England and was hung in celebration of the 50th anniversary of William Penn's charter of liberty for the province of Pennsylvania in 1701. The freedom message and Bible verse, *"Proclaim liberty throughout all the land unto all the inhabitants thereof"* (Leviticus 25:10), was already on the bell when it was tolled for liberty at the signing of our Declaration of Independence in 1776. When it was excitedly rung for the first time ever that glorious day, it split apart.) Also on that day, Congress selected Thomas Jefferson, John Adams, and Benjamin Franklin to form the committee that would design the United States great seal. Benjamin Franklin suggested the seal be *"Moses lifting up his wand, and dividing the red sea, and pharaoh in his chariot overwhelmed with the waters,"* and the motto become *"Rebellion to tyrants is obedience to God."* He thought this best characterized the spirit of our new nation. Thomas Jefferson proposed, *"The children of Israel in the wilderness, led by a cloud by day, and a pillar of fire by night."*

Sharing the excitement that was surging through the colonies, Pastor Samuel West of Massachusetts reflected after the Declaration of Independence had been signed, *"I cannot help hoping, and even believing, that Providence has designed this continent for to be the asylum of liberty and true religion."*

On July 9, Congress established prayer as a daily part to remind them from whence their help came. Also, they authorized the Continental Army to provide chaplains for their troops. Furthermore, General Washington issued the order to appoint chaplains to every regiment. In his first general order to his troops, he called on *"every officer and man…to live, and act, as becomes a Christian Soldier defending the dearest Rights and Liberties of his country."*

LONG ISLAND & NEW YORK CITY

After the British fled from Boston, Washington believed that they might attempt to overtake Long Island. He began to make a defensive strategy to fortify New York City and the surrounding area from a British invasion, since it was a vital link between New England and the southern colonies. Since the British might strike anywhere, the Continental Army was stretched thin as they constructed trenches, forts, obstacles, and gun batteries across the countryside.

On June 25, 1776, three British warships sudden appeared in the haze of the New York Bay. A few days later, over one hundred more vessels joined them, and British soldiers began to encamp on

Staten Island. By mid-August, reinforcements came from England, creating the largest military force ever deployed overseas by the British Empire at that time – over 400 vessels and 32,000 troops including thousands of German mercenaries called "Hessians." King George III and Parliament desired to destroy the "American rebels" with one decisive blow and regain control of the colonies quickly. At this sight, Private Daniel McCurtin of the Maryland Rifles recorded in his diary, *"I declare, at my noticing this, that I could not believe my eyes…. In about ten minutes the whole bay was full of shipping as ever it could be…. I thought all London was afloat."*

The colonists were growing restless; the British were planning something BIG. With the British about to attack, George Washington told his men, *"The fate of the unborn millions will now depend, under God, on the courage and conduct of this army. Let us, therefore, rely upon the goodness of the cause and the aid of the Supreme Being, in whose hands victory is, to animate and encourage us to great and noble actions."*

On August 22, 1776, it began; the British began to take position on Long Island. The few thousand American troops tried to build obstacles and felled trees to slow down the British advance, but they made no attempt to cover their flanks, thinking that the British would come with a straightforward attack.

British General Howe made careful plans to try and outwit the Continental Army, having learned his lesson well at Bucker Hill. He learned about the colonists' defensive measures and plans from Loyalist informants (Americans against the War for Independence and completely "loyal" to the king). As the attack commenced, Howe directed a portion of his army to preoccupy the colonists with a frontal assault; meanwhile, with the bulk of his troops, he compromised the American's left flank quickly and quietly. Not expecting this maneuver, the Continental Army only dispatched five officers on horseback to continually scout out their flanks and provide warning of any British activity that might occur. However, all five officers were captured before they were able to warn Washington and his men.

As the British began to overrun the colonists' positions, men began to retreat, seeing that it was impossible to fight in two different directions and that many regiments were quickly being surrounded and forced to surrender. Providentially, the British did not pursue the Continental Army as they should have for a final, devastating blow; rather, General Howe ordered his army to halt. His subordinates pleaded with him to allow them to continue pressing forward; but he refused, being hesitant of what lay ahead.

Furthermore, he was confident that the Continental Army was essentially trapped on the western end of Long Island, since his brother Admiral Dick Howe was waiting on the East River with his squadron of warships to gun them down and cut them off from escaping. However, during this time, the wind had shifted from its normal southeastern breeze along the New York coast to a violent northeasterly gale, making it impossible for the British ships to stay in position. This northeasterly gust brought in a powerful storm of high winds and heavy rains from August 27 to August 29.

Little did General Howe realize, if he *had* continued his advance on August 27, he would have crushed a major portion of the Continental Army and also captured most of its leaders, including General George Washington himself; but now the weather immobilized both armies. On August 29 under the disguise provided by the weather, Washington ordered a masterful retreat to Manhattan Island using the Brooklyn ferry landing. The Army made its way to the shore, loaded supplies into vessels to be taken across the river through the darkness, and evacuated the newest troops first to the veterans last. A small task force of brave colonists remained behind at the deserted camp to keep the fires burning brightly and to make it sound as if the troops were still restlessly holding their position until about 6:00 AM the next morning.

Crossing the East River seemed to be impossible with the weather and tide very unfavorable that evening. The commander in charge of the evacuation operation ordered one of his subordinates to find George Washington and ask him to reconsider and delay the order. Providentially, Washington could not be found; soon after, the wind died down, making it easier to move the full boats across the river and allowing the evacuation to continue on schedule.

A certain Mr. and Mrs. John Repelye lived near the Brooklyn ferry landing where the colonists were secretly conducting their escape. Because the Continental Army believed they were Loyalists, they decided to temporarily detain Mr. Repelye so he would not be able to alert the British of the Army's evacuation. During the middle of the night, Mrs. Repelye secretly sent out her Negro servant to inform any British officer he could find about the "rebels'" undercover plans. After he successfully worked his way past the colonists' defensive lines, the servant was captured by a Hessian patrol. Not being able to understand English or any of the servant's urgent news, they concluded that he must have been part of the Continental Army, despite the man's pleas, and kept him as their prisoner. When he finally was able to explain his information to a British officer the next morning, it was too late.

As the British arrived at Brooklyn ferry landing, Washington (who had determined to be the last off Long Island) and the remainder of his troops pushed off shore and disappeared into the thick fog that shrouded the East River. Though the British opened fire on these last boats to leave, they lost them in the midst of this supernatural occurrence.

Major Benjamin Tallmadge, one of those who were last to leave with Washington, described: *"As the dawn of the next day approached, those of us who remained in the trenches became very anxious for our own safety, and when the dawn appeared there were several regiments still on duty. At this time a very dense fog began to rise, and it seemed to settle in a peculiar manner over both encampments. I recollect this peculiar providential occurrence perfectly well; and so very dense was the atmosphere that I could scarcely discern a man at six yards distance."* The fog that intervened at this instance was called the "heavenly messenger." According to eyewitnesses and citizens of the area, a fog of this magnitude during that season had not been seen for over twenty to thirty years. Major Tallmadge concluded, *"The providential appearance of the fog saved a part of our army from being captured, and certainly myself among other who formed the rear guard."* Truly, the Continental Army was under the protection of the Divine Providence, as they pleaded to be in the Declaration of Independence.

When Great Britain received the news of their victory in Long Island and New York, celebration commenced, bells rang, and cannons were fired. The King proudly pronounced that they had won the war. However, though the Continental Army was greatly crippled and barely escaped from the grasp of the British, the American patriots had no plans to quit. Though the colonists' morale was low, they would not give up that easily. If the British wanted victory, they would have to get it the hard way.

TRENTON, NEW JERSEY

After the retreat from Long Island in August of 1777, the Continental Army attempted to hold their ground against the British time and time again, but they could only continue to retreat across the New England colonies to avoid disaster. Men were growing discouraged, and, unfortunately, many were abandoning their posts in the Army. Washington wrote to his brother Augustine, *"If every nerve is not strained to recruit the new army with all possible expedition, I think the game is pretty nearly up.... You can form no idea of the perplexity of my situation. No man, I believe, ever had a greater choice of difficulties, and less means to extricate himself from them."*

However, on September 11, Congress approved and recommended to the American people that 20,000 Bibles be imported and distributed among the troops to improve their morale as they went "through the valley of the shadow of death." This move by our Founding Fathers was vastly essential in binding the hearts of the Continental Army to their common cause – fighting for life, liberty, and the pursuit of happiness, freedoms given to them by God Himself. Thomas Paine, who was with the Army during this time, wrote, *"These are the times that try men's souls. The summer soldier and sunshine patriot will, in this crisis, shrink from the service of his country; but he that stands it now, deserves the love and thanks of every man and woman."*

By December, Washington found himself across the river from Trenton, New Jersey with only three thousand men. The Continental Army was short of men, material, supplies, food, ammunition, and clothing. As winter increased, sickness began to spread wildly among the ranks of soldiers. Nevertheless, before Washington lay a courageous opportunity: he viewed the Hessian stronghold at Trenton of 1,400 soldiers commanded by Colonel Johann Rall as a possible point of victory. He believed that through God's help, it could and would be done.

Ever since the Hessians had arrived in Trenton and decided to encamp there for the winter, on several occasions small groups of minutemen would attack their patrols. To the Hessians, these "rebels" were a nuisance and an irritating thorn in their flesh. Both Colonel Rall's subordinates and superior recommended to him to take all precaution against these Americans and to set up fortifications around Trenton. However, Rall ignored the instructions and advice he was given, too caught up in his own confidence and contempt for the "weak" colonists. He exclaimed proudly, *"Let them come! We want no trenches! We'll at them with the bayonet!"*

Though Washington prepared his daring plan – to cross the Delaware River on Christmas night with 2,400 soldiers – in secrecy, word of his bold attack got out several days before as two deserters of the Continental Army warned the Hessians that militia units were gathering in Pennsylvania with Washington to advance on their position. The Hessians had plenty of time to prepare themselves for it. On December 23, after receiving word from a Negro who just crossed the Delaware River and noticed the colonists gathering and preparing to launch a surprise attack on Trenton, Dr. William Bryant sought out Colonel Rall and informed him of the rising danger. British General James Grant at Princeton, New Jersey, also forwarded to Rall intelligence reports of an attack on Christmas Day.

The Hessians were not worried; only one of their three regiments was on standby, ready for an engagement. Around 7:00 PM, firing broke out on the north side of town as the Hessian outpost of Pennington Road came under attack. Rall immediately sent reinforcements to strengthen this position and to repel back the colonist offensive; the rest of his garrison bristled with readiness. After the Hessians first intensive volley of returned fire, the unknown group of colonists broke off the attack and disbanded throughout the forest. A Hessian patrol went up Pennington Road for two miles but found no sign of these men. The Christmas day attack seemed to be over. After he discovered that there were only thirty American "rebels" who comprised this "Christmas day attack force" – he laughed and shrugged off the concern of a major Continental Army advance, imagining that the information had been blown out of proportion.

When he returned to Trenton, Rall informed his men that the threat was over, and ordered them to return to their quarters because of the miserable weather and enjoy the Christmas celebrations to their fullest. Late that night, Rall and his troops were playing cards and consuming much alcohol when a Loyalist farmer came a long distance from Pennsylvania to warn them of the true attack upon Trenton that would soon come. When he finally found out where Rall was, he beat on the door repeatedly and begged the servant who opened it to let him speak with the Hessian colonel. The servant would not let him in, insisting that the colonel was too busy to "deal" with him. So, in the midst of the cold, snowy evening, the farmer wrote out a note explaining how the entire Continental Army was crossing the Delaware River to launch a surprise attack in the early dawn. The servant gave the note to Rall, who glanced at it, saw it written in English, and did not bother having someone translate it for him. Rather, he crumpled up the valuable letter, stuffed it into his pocket, and continued playing cards.

As Washington and his men climbed into their vessels and ferried across the treacherous, ice-filled waters of the Delaware River, they were oblivious of how God had already supernaturally intervened on their behalf multiple times over the week. In the beginning of the morning, the Continental Army stormed into Trenton and caught the Hessian garrison by complete surprise. In the confusion, Colonel Rall was mortally wounded while trying to rally his men to fight. As he lay dying in a pool of blood, someone found the Loyalist farmer's note given to him the night before still in his pocket. When he was informed of its valuable contents, he said, *"If I had read this...I would not be here now."* Truly, the events of that morning would have occurred in a completely different way.

By 9:00AM, the battle was over. Washington with his men were providentially victorious and were able to obtain a large supply of greatly needed equipment, ammunition, and artillery. With their morale greatly boosted, the Continental Army was also able to win a strategic victory against the British at Princeton a few days later.

Full of ingenuity, bravery, and tenacity, our Founding Fathers and the American patriots refused to stop, quit, or lay down their arms, because they fought for something worth dying for. These much-needed victories at Trenton and Princeton, combined with the miraculous victories the following year over the British and Hessian forces at Saratoga, New York, brought regiments of recruits to join the Continental Army and convinced France to assist the American colonies in their struggle for freedom. Soon, the American coasts would be patrolled by French warships, harbors would be docked with French frigates loaded full of supplies, and French soldiers would be fighting with them in their cause for independence. In spite of the desperate circumstances the colonists faced, God was smiling upon the United States of America.

THE WINTER AT VALLEY FORGE

During the winter of 1777-1778, the Continental Army settled at Valley Forge, Pennsylvania. Washington chose this location because it seemed to be close enough to the British to keep their raiding parties out of the interior of Pennsylvania, yet far enough away to halt the threat of any surprise attacks. The conditions were so severe at times that Washington grieved *"that unless some great and capital change suddenly takes place… this Army must inevitably….Starve, dissolve, or disperse, in order to obtain subsistence in the best manner they can."*

Here, Washington's trust in God was really put to the test as he watched his own men endure hardship during the cold, bitter winter without appropriate equipment, food, or clothing. In the midst of the cold afternoons, Washington began to pour himself out before God with a broken heart in isolated locations in the woods. In an amazing account, a Quaker man named Isaac Potts who opposed the "violence" of the War for Independence said that he *"never believed that America c'd proceed against Great Britain whose fleets and armies covered the land and ocean, but something very extraordinary converted me to the Good Faith!"* On one cold wintery day, as he was quietly riding through the woods, he relates: *"I heard a plaintive sound as, of a man at prayer. I tied my horse to a sapling and went quietly into the woods and to my astonishment I saw the great George Washington on his knees alone, with his sword on one side and his cocked hat on the other. He was at Prayer to the God of the Armies, beseeching to interpose with his Divine aid, as it was ye Crisis, and the cause of the country, of humanity and of the world. Such a prayer I never heard from the lips of man. I left him alone praying. I went home and told my wife. I saw a sight and heard...what I never saw or heard before, and just related to her what I had seen and heard and observed. We never thought a man c'd be a soldier and a Christian, but if there is one in the world, it is Washington. She also was astonished. We thought it was the cause of God, and America could prevail."* **America did prevail in the end!**

Though he made this amazing discovery, Potts had no intention of seeking out Washington in the midst of his private, fervent prayer. However, Potts' story shows how often Washington poured out his heart to God and depended upon His guidance, discernment, and power to carry them through to victory with safety.

Though things were looking somewhat bright for the colonists, the war would last for another five years. For Washington and his men a decisive victory had been won that winter – a victory not of weapons but of will, creating a heart determined to depend upon God no matter what. Because of the faith of soldiers like General George Washington, God chose to providentially guide and protect the Continental Army.

WEST POINT, NEW YORK

In September, 1780, Continental General Benedict Arnold had grown very bitter at Congress for not promoting him in the Army and for never fulfilling their promise to pay him back a portion of the wealth he had already spent on the American cause. Therefore, he decided to secretly sell out the Continental Army to the enemy for a large sum of money and to defect to Britain's cause soon after. He secretly met with British Major Andrea and gave him important war information, strategic in bringing a decisive British victory over the American forces. While attempting to take these secrets back to his headquarters, Major Andrea came to a fork in the road, and he did not know which direction to turn to get back to the British lines. If he had gone to the right, he would have made it safely to where his regiments were encamped. Instead, he nonchalantly flipped a coin, and decided to go to the left. Whom do you think he encountered? That's right – the American Colonists. Clearly, it was God's Providence.

THE BATTLE OF YORKTOWN

As this "American Revolution" continued to drag on, many in England felt that necessary actions were not being taken in dealing with the Continental Army. Many believed that British time, money, and energy were being wasted by chasing these "rebels" across the countryside, and that these "traitors" should be conquered swiftly in a straight-forward manner (in the form of fighting they understood). As the American colonies were now beginning to receive sympathy and support from other nations around the world, Great Britain became increasingly uncertain if they could truly win the war. However, King George III remained unchanged in his proud, hardened heart. He was determined to defeat this "rebellion" at whatever cost and continued to urge Parliament and his cabinet to maintain firm action. Agitated and irritated, Parliament began to consider whether or not the British generals in the colonies were really the best choice for the positions. As they investigated and decided who might be fit for the command, in May of 1778, Henry Clinton replaced General Howe as the commander-in-chief of the British/Hessians forces occupying the American colonies.

From December, 1779, through 1780, Generals Clinton and Cornwallis with their combined armies won stunning victories at Charleston and Camden in the Southern colonies. The Continental Army was decimated, now facing their lowest point in the war since December, 1776, when they had fled from New York. Clinton stationed his troops in New York City and remained posed for any colonial offensive in the north. However, now that France had entered the war and began to show signs of offensive activity in the Caribbean, both generals recognized that they needed to secure a base toward the heart of the colonies on the eastern coastline so their forces could easily shift north or south as the war continued to play out.

Providentially, on May 31, 1781, British intelligence intercepted a letter that George Washington wrote to French General Lafayette describing detailed plans proposing a combined French and American attack on New York City. A short time later, Washington changed his mind when he secretly surveyed the solid British defenses around the city. He wrote in his diary, *"I could scarce see a ground upon which to continue my preparations against New York."*

However, the hand of God was once again at work on the behalf of the American patriots. After receiving this valuable information about the colonists' battle plans, General Clinton became quite fearful of a surprising American victory. Therefore, he nervously began to take extreme action in a rather indecisive way. Along with installing several new defensive positions, he sent orders to Cornwallis on June 11 to send six infantry battalions and any extra artillery and cavalry units that could be spared to help defend New York City from the anticipated attack. On June 26, Clinton then issued new orders sending these reinforcements to Philadelphia, to hold their position there instead of coming all the way to New York. Finally, he directed Cornwallis to recall all of these troops and to secure a naval base on the Chesapeake as they had originally planned. These series of events caused Cornwallis to secure a central location in the colonies on the bottle-necked peninsula of Yorktown, Virginia. Here, he waited in frustration for the arrival of British naval support and further orders. This great confusion was providentially used to the Continental Army's advantage.

Finding out what Cornwallis had hastily done and that the French navy would soon be approaching the Chesapeake Bay with over fifty-five warships loaded with fresh troops, Washington began marching toward Virginia with the majority of his Continental/French armies. He left only a portion of his men behind after establishing a false camp in New Jersey, attempting to deceive the British in New York that he was preparing to pounce with a surprise attack on Staten Island. Washington's ploy worked.

As the British navy arrived in the Chesapeake Bay with Cornwallis's support and reinforcements, in perfect, providential timing, the French fleets from the North Atlantic and the Caribbean (over 1,500 miles apart) arrived, enabling an overwhelming French victory. The British were forced to withdraw, leaving Cornwallis surrounded by the French navy in the Bay and American/French troops around Yorktown.

It was not until late September that Clinton discovered he had been outsmarted by Washington and that Cornwallis was in a very difficult position. He sent Cornwallis a letter of assurance to not give up any ground and to expect a large number of reinforcements *"in a few days."* However, Clinton was very slow in assembling the men and equipment to aid Cornwallis. By October, one British staff officer wrote in his journal, *"If the Navy are not a little more active they will not get a sight of the Capes of Virginia before the end of the month, and then it will be a little too late."*

Exasperated, Cornwallis pulled back his troops into the inner defensive positions of Yorktown as the overwhelming Continental and French forces continued to advance. Meanwhile, British scouts discovered that there would be very little resistance from the colonists if they successfully crossed the York River in the Chesapeake Bay and headed north under the cover of night. In one final attempt to break free, Cornwallis and his men obtained every available vessel along the coast and hastily began around midnight. However, before the boats could return from ferrying across the first wave of troops, a strong storm arose with violent winds, scattering the vessels down the river and stopping the undercover operation. Observers from that night relate that it was as severe a storm as they had ever remembered experiencing.

After this, Cornwallis knew that he had nowhere to turn. God had shut them down. The next morning, a British officer walked out from the trenches waving a white flag. A few days later, on October 19, 1781, Cornwallis officially surrendered. Ironically, on that same day, the British Navy finally departed from New York City with Clinton's reinforcements; they arrived one week too late.

The Americans had won, and all were able now to focus on eradicating Clinton from New York City. Within six months, Parliament voted to end the war in America and six months after that, initial peace treaties were signed. The War for Independence quickly and providentially came to an end. America became an independent, newborn nation.

CONCLUSION

In the Declaration of Independence, our Founding Fathers begged for God, as the Supreme Judge of the universe, to evaluate the prosecution and tyranny of Great Britain and the defense and motive of the American Colonies and to favor the side of the right. Throughout the War for Independence, without a doubt, we can clearly see how God guided and aided the American colonies in their brave fight for freedom. Obviously, He would help the country that lived by Psalm 33:12 which teaches, *"Blessed is the nation whose God is the LORD; and the people whom he hath chosen for his own inheritance."*

When Washington became our first President under the new Constitution of the United States, he said in his Inaugural Address:

"No people can be bound to acknowledge and adore the Invisible Hand which conducts the affairs of men more than the people of the United States. Every step by which they have advanced to the character of an independent nation seems to have been distinguished by some token of providential agency... We ought to be no less persuaded that the propitious smiles of Heaven can never be expected on a nation that disregards the eternal rules of order and right which Heaven itself has ordained."

And through his final words, Washington challenged the people of America to unite as one nation under God, pointing out that this nation would only continue to prosper if they would follow what He had ordained in His Word. The Bible clearly projects in Proverbs 14:34, *"Righteousness exalteth a nation: but sin is a reproach to any people."* Psalm 144:15 reveals, *"Happy is that people, that is in such a case: yea, happy is that people, whose God is the LORD."*

THE BLACK REGIMENT
Colonial Preachers, their Preaching, & their Patriotism

During the beginning of 18th century, God began to work spiritually in the hearts and minds of the colonists of America. The flames of revival burned brightly up and down the eastern seaboard by the middle of the 1700's. Thousands would amass together, hungry for the truth of God's Word. Through the preaching of Jonathan Edwards and Isaac Backus in New England, Baptist preacher Shubal Stearns in the Southern colonies, John Wesley and George Whitefield traveling throughout the entirety of the colonies, and countless unnamed "circuit riding" evangelists, tens of thousands of Americans were converted and began to live their lives and raise their families by the Bible. Benjamin Franklin reflected as he saw this "Great Awakening" sweep across the thirteen colonies, *"It was wonderful to see the change soon made in the manners of our inhabitants. From being thoughtless or indifferent about religion, it seemed as if all the world were growing religious, so that one could not walk through the town in an evening without hearing psalms sung in different families of every street."* Without a doubt, the *Great Awakening* (as it soon became commonly called) was a key factor in uniting the separate pre-Revolutionary War colonies and in increasing communication among them.

However, liberals and revisionist historians are trying to hide how the preaching of God's Word during our War for Independence was one of the key elements that created the spirit of independence among our founding fathers. Preachers would strongly stand behind their pulpits, unashamed and with great courage, and would boldly preach against the tyranny of Great Britain, telling their parishioners that they had the right to walk out onto the field of battle and defend their homes. These preachers across the colonies *"dealt in no high sounding phrases of liberty and equality; they went to the veer foundations of society, showed what the natural rights of man were, and how those rights became modified when men gathered into communities; how all laws and regulations were designed to be for the good of the governed; that the object of concentrated power was to protect not invade personal liberty, and when it failed to do this, and oppressed instead of protected, assailed instead of defended rights, resistance became lawful, nay, obligatory. They showed also the nature of compacts and charters, and applied the whole subject to the case of the Colonies"* (*The Chaplains and Clergy of the Revolution* by J.T. Headley, page 4). They would get to the heart of the matter concerning life, the essence of liberty, and the rights of the colonists in their controversy with Great Britain.

God's men intensely fought for freedom and debated the points of liberty in Independence Hall and Continental Congress. Their preaching was responsible for setting aflame the hearts of the America people for independence and freedom.

Newspapers back then were more of a "novelty" than a consistent source of news and political views. Therefore, the pulpit was the most direct and effectual way to reach the people. The Massachusetts House of Representatives knew this and so they passed a resolution requesting the preachers of their state *"to make the question of the rights of the Colonies and the oppressive conduct of the mother country a topic of the pulpit on week days."* (ibid.) Furthermore, up and down the colonies, pastors would often print their political sermons and pass out their pamphlets on Sundays when their churches were flocked with people. These messages quickly spread across their counties and *"became the text books of human rights in every parish."* (ibid.)

This primarily ignited the flame of patriotism and true liberty in the hearts of our forefathers. These heroic men became known abroad and referred to by the British as the **BLACK REGIMENT**, since most of them wore a black vesture when they preached in the pulpit. Famous Loyalist (an English sympathizer) Peter Oliver of the colonies complained that these men were *"invariably at the heart of revolutionary disturbances."*

The preacher was usually the best educated man and most informed individual in his community. They were men of resilient testimonies with fiery dispositions. John Adams observed, *"The Philadelphia ministers thunder and lighten every Sabbath against George III's despotism."* Thomas Jefferson reflected, observing his native colony of Virginia, *"Pulpit oratory ran like a shock of electricity through the whole colony."*

Pastor Jonathan Mayhew created the famous phrase *"no taxation without representation."* In 1765, after King George III passed the Stamp Act, Pastor Mayhew reasoned with the American people from the pulpit and through pamphlet: *"The king is as much bound by his oath not to infringe the legal rights of the people, as the people are bound to yield subjection to him. From whence it follows that as soon as the prince set himself above the law, he loses the king in the tyrant. He does, to all intent and purposes, un-king himself."* He urged the necessity of colonial union to secure colonial liberties. His preaching was greatly heard and introduced the ideas of *"the cause of liberty"* and *"the right and duty to resist tyranny."* His sermons were widely read throughout the colonies.

Pastor Sam Davies of Virginia declared, *"Is it not our duty, in the sight of God, is it not a work to which the Lord loudly calls us, to take up arms for the defense of our country?"*

In early 1776, Pastor Peter Muhlenberg of Woodstock, VA, called upon the men of his congregation to join him in fighting for our nation's independence. He preached from the book of Ecclesiastics that there was a time for peace and a time for war, *"In the language of the Holy Writ, there is a time for all things, a time to preach and a time to pray, but those times have passed away...there is a time to fight – and that time has now come!"* Contending that the time of war had arrived, Muhlenberg then concluded his sermon by casting off his black clerical robes to reveal the uniform of a Continental Army officer. He stepped down from his pulpit and walked out the church down the center aisle. Many men stood and boldly walked out with him to serve with their pastor. When his brother Fredrick Muhlenberg, a pastor in New York, found out what Peter had done in Virginia, he wrote him a letter and rebuked him, saying that it was unwise of him to leave his church and take up arms. He encouraged his brother Peter that he should attempt a more peaceful means of rebelling against the tyranny of Great Britain. However, when the British came through, ransacked, and destroyed his church, Fredrick Muhlenberg realized his brother Peter was right and very eagerly engaged himself in the struggle for liberty.

Though surrounded by Tories (Americans who were sympathetic toward the crown and were against the War for Independence) all about him and his church throughout his Huntington, Connecticut, community, Pastor David Ely preached against the tyranny of Britain so greatly that the Tories declared that if the "Rebellion" was squelched, they would raid his home and hang him on the oak tree that was in the front of his church.

In Duxbury, Massachusetts, seventy-six year old Pastor Joseph Fish, had the opportunity to address the public at their town meeting after George Washington sent out the general plea for volunteers to join the Continental Army. Lifting up his frail voice with a fire in his bones, he proclaimed, *"Were it not that my nerves are unstrung, and my limbs enfeebled with age, on such a call as you have, I think I should willingly quit the desk, put off my priestly garments, buckle on the harness, and, with trumpet in hand, hasten to battle."*

Pastor Jonah Stearns of New Hampshire not only preached independence throughout his community, but sacrificed nearly everything for it and to give aid to Washington's needy men.

The British came to the home and property of Pastor David Cauldwell of Pennsylvania and greedily plundered it, along with burning all the books from his library and his family's furniture in the front yard. He was hunted across the country as a fugitive because of his boldness behind the pulpit and his devotion for liberty.

In 1776, Pennsylvania Pastor Thomas Read, along with forty to fifty of his men, formed a small militia, shouldered their muskets, and marched to Philadelphia to help the Continental Army defend itself against the invasion of British General Howe. Because of his knowledge of the shortcuts throughout the countryside, the following year Pastor Read saved the life of General Washington and many of his men from being overtaken and captured by the enemy at Elk Ferry.

Pastor Samuel Spring was used of God in a great way to keep the spirits and morale of the men high. He preached soul-stirring messages every weekend, and when their rations were low and disease was breaking out among them, he would make a pulpit out of the men's knapsacks and preach encouraging, uplifting sermons of the everlasting Gospel of Jesus Christ.

Bro. Samuel Payson of Chelsea, Massachusetts, preached directly against any type of bloodshed, violence, and the horrors of war. He heralded throughout his communities that it was our duty not to resist but to be patient and even remain in submission to the government no matter how drastic the tyranny was. Because of his strong stand against his fellow preachers (who were urging their congregations to take up arms and defend their homes), his brethren refused to let him preach in their pulpits, afraid that he would spread his "heresy." However, after the battle of Lexington and the brutality of the British hitting close to his home, his eyes were opened and his outlook miraculously changed. Enraged, this peaceful pastor grabbed the musket he owned, joined the local militia that was forming, and became the leader of it. As they left Chelsea to join with other militias forming into a "Continental Army," they discovered a large number of British soldiers nearby. With great courage, he compelled his men to advance and face their foe. Standing steady and unashamed, they caught the British by surprise and fired destructive volley after volley into them. The entire enemy was slain except for a few who were captured.

Pastor William Graham of Paxton, Pennsylvania, when he saw the hesitance and sensed the unwillingness of a number of the young men from his community to enlist in a company of riflemen, stepped out of the crowd toward the enrollment table and stated that though he was an old man, he would be more than willing to walk out onto the field of battle. Somewhat embarrassed, the young men also came and enlisted because of his example.

Pastor John Steele of Cumberland, Pennsylvania, served as a captain in the Continental Army and often led the advance company of nine hundred men to the front lines. He always preached with his gun by his side – leaning against a tree or the pulpit.

During a pressing confrontation with the British, Pastor Azel Roe's regiment began to retreat and cower away from the front lines. In enraged desperation, he ran out onto the battlefield in front of the British – putting himself in grave danger in order to get the attention of his troops. Turning around and seeing this "crazed" act, the men pleaded for him to take cover and retreat with them, but he refused. With musket balls whizzing past him, he demanded that they come back and continue to fight it out with the British.

Pastor Nathaniel Porter commonly marched with the troops, encouraging them and sustaining their fight for liberty, through the wilderness to Fort Independence on Lake Champlain.

During a dangerous small pox epidemic, Pastor Amnie Robbins, from Branford, Massachusetts, was one of only a few men in his brigade who had not yet become ill. Although he was not a trained medical doctor, he willingly volunteered to nurse his fellow soldiers back to health. He selflessly sat by their bedside, praying with them and offering any medical assistance he could, until they had all begun to recover. It was then that Pastor Robbins became ill with the small pox and did not survive, passing away shortly thereafter.

Pastor Samuel McClintock of Greenland, New Hampshire, fought side by side with the troops at the Battle of Bunker Hill in his clerical robes. He later encouraged his four sons to join the fight in the war for independence. Only one survived.

Pastor Thomas Allen bravely stated to his troops before battle, *"Rather than quit this ground with infamy and disgrace, I should prefer leaving this body of mine a corpse on the spot."*

Pastor Hezekiah Ripley, a personal friend of Washington, was often seen stooping over the beds of the sick and dying, praying with them in their hour of need. Because of his inspiring messages, he was a favored preacher among the troops. One morning, after hearing the news that his house, furniture and library had been burnt to the ground by British raiders, he refused to sigh and regret his decision to fight for freedom, no matter what sacrifices he would have to make.

When the British attempted to land close to their homes, Pastor Isaac Lewis assembled the men of his congregation to join him in repelling these invaders, standing together near the shore with their muskets aimed at the enemy. As the British attacked, a cannon ball landed within three feet of Lewis, but he never flinched. He only emboldened his men to keep fighting. Eventually, they were forced to retreat due to the overwhelming numbers of their enemy. The men gathered their families and some of their possessions and took refuge until the danger had passed. Then Pastor Lewis, gathering the people into a house so remote the British would not find them, preached a sermon from Isaiah 64:11-12 that greatly encouraged their hearts.

Pastor John Martin, after praying with the soldiers at Bunker Hill, seized his musket and fought gallantly to the close of the battle. A couple of days later, he preached to the remaining men in his shattered regiment from Nehemiah 4:14, *"And I said unto the nobles and to the rulers, and to the rest of the people, be ye not afraid of them."*

Pastor Nathaniel Bartlett lived in Reading but had church members in both Reading and Putnam. Whenever he traveled to meet with his parishioners in Putnam, he carried a loaded rifle, in case he needed to defend himself against the Tories who had sworn to hang him if he was ever caught. Despite the death threat looming over his head, Pastor Bartlett never abandoned his Putnam church, traveling many dangerous miles as often as he could to visit his people. Because of his faithfulness and bravery, God always protected him. Bartlett never even had to fire his rifle.

Because of his political position and the influence he had on the people, during a British raid, sharpshooters snuck into the backyard of Pastor James Caldwell's home, and shot and killed his wife through the bedroom window. Thinking that this heinous crime would deter him, it only emboldened him to preach stronger and continue on the battlefield. He found the biggest Bible he could and would always slam it down on the pulpit. He would lay two braces of pistols on either side of it and dared for the British to come and try to take his Bible or his guns away from him and stop him from preaching. One day as they were on the field of battle, the troops ran out of paper wadding for their muskets – Caldwell galloped over to the nearby church and started grabbing hymnals. Riding back to the front lines with eyes wide with excitement, he flung them out to the troops and screamed, *"Give 'em, Watts, boys! Give 'em Watts!"* (since most of the songs in the book were written by the famous musician, Isaac Watts.)

David Jones, a Baptist preacher patriot, was greatly trusted by Washington and was appointed chaplain of Colonel St. Clair's regiment and was at the battle of Ticonderoga. He also served under General Gates and General "Mad" Anthony Wayne. He preached repentance and independence among the troops to encourage their hearts, but he also was a fierce fighter on the battle field. At the battle of Brandywine, as he rode in the midst of the fighting, his horse was shot out from under him. Jumping to his feet after he had been throne off his animal, he continued to shoot at the enemy. And then when his ammunition would not fire, with sheer valor and courage, he flung his pistol in the face of the nearest of the advancing troops and continued to fight. He miraculously survived without injury and then continued serving at Valley Forge with Washington and to the end of the war when Cornwallis surrendered at Yorktown.

John Gano pastored in New York City, where – unknown to him – Washington would sit outside the open window of his Baptist church and listen to this young man's fervent, heart-filled preaching. Impressed with his passion and testimony, Washington chose him as his personal chaplain. Often, Gano would be found working among the wounded on the battle field to assure their eternal destiny with them, but many times he would also be found on the front lines sharing the soldiers' perils and eagerly pushing forward with them. General Washington said that Baptist chaplains like John Gano were *"the most prominent and useful in the Army."* When the War for Independence was finally over and the British flag was being lowered at Yorktown and Old Glory was rising on the flag pole to take its place, Washington turned to Gano and asked him to give the final prayer of thanksgiving for God granting them the victory.

Men of God stood shoulder-to-shoulder with our founding fathers, involved with politics and the ratification of our Constitution and courageously fighting with them on the field of battle. Without question, the preaching, leadership, wisdom, and testimony of God's men were hailed throughout the colonies as the spark which ignited victory and patriotism.

"All these, and a hundred other great and good men, by their example and eloquence fed the fires of liberty, and sustained the courage of the people. Men of learning and culture, they were looked up to for advice and counsel — whose praise was not only in all the churches, but throughout the land, for their integrity, ability, and patriotism. These formed a host of devoted laborers in the common cause, but more than this, their prayers rose incessantly, from camp and field, that God would defend the right, and save His people. These last are counted as nothing by the historian, but we may rest assured that they did more than resolutions of Congress, and acts of committees of safety, towards achieving our liberties. One may consider it beneath the dignity of history to put them among the causes that led ultimately to our success: but when that history comes to be read in the light of eternity, the enthusiasm of volunteers and the steady courage of the disciplined battalions, will sink into insignificance beside the devoted prayers and faith of these men of God." (Headley, pages 20-21)

American preachers were responsible for providing the conviction and wisdom necessary for winning a war against the cruelty of an unjust government. This **BLACK REGIMENT** would ascend to their pulpits day after day and preach and instill into the hearts of our founding fathers and fighting patriots the sacred fire of the War for Independence, knowing that they were fighting against tyranny. Without the tenacious courage exhibited by the preachers of the Black Regiment in the pulpit, in the countryside, in Continental Congress, and on the battlefield — would have American independence ever been achieved? It is very doubtful. The preaching of the Bible and true Godly spirit of patriotism was the fuel that kept America marching forward. America became the successful nation that it did because of the fiery preaching within the pulpit.

America was once the greatest Christian nation on the face of the earth. Alexis de Tocqueville was a famous 19th century French statesman, historian and social philosopher. He traveled to America in the 1830's to discover the reasons for the incredible success of this new nation. He published his observations in his classic two-volume work, Democracy in America. He was especially impressed by America's religious character. Here are some startling excerpts from Tocqueville's great work:

Upon my arrival in the United States the religious aspect of the country was the first thing that struck my attention; and the longer I stayed there, the more I perceived the great political consequences resulting from this new state of things.

In France I had almost always seen the spirit of religion and the spirit of freedom marching in opposite directions. But in America I found they were intimately united and that they reigned in common over the same country.

Religion in America...must be regarded as the foremost of the political institutions of that country; for if it does not impart a taste for freedom, it facilitates the use of it. Indeed, it is in this same point of view that the inhabitants of the United States themselves look upon religious belief.

I do not know whether all Americans have a sincere faith in their religion – for who can search the human heart? But I am certain that they hold it to be indispensable to the maintenance of republican institutions. This opinion is not peculiar to a class of citizens or a party, but it belongs to the whole nation and to every rank of society.

In the United States, the sovereign authority is religious...there is no country in the world where the Christian religion retains a greater influence over the souls of men than in America, and there can be no greater proof of its utility and of its conformity to human nature than that its influence is powerfully felt over the most enlightened and free nation of the earth.

In the United States, the influence of religion is not confined to the manners, but it extends to the intelligence of the people...

Christianity, therefore, reigns without obstacle, by universal consent...

I sought for the key to the greatness and genius of America in her harbors...; in her fertile fields and boundless forests; in her rich mines and vast world commerce; in her public school system and institutions of learning. I sought for it in her democratic Congress and in her matchless Constitution.

Not until I went into the churches of America and heard her pulpits flame with righteousness did I understand the secret of her genius and power.

America is great because America is good, and if America ever ceases to be good, America will cease to be great.

The safeguard of morality is religion, and morality is the best security of law as well as the surest pledge of freedom.

The Americans combine the notions of Christianity and of liberty so intimately in their minds, that it is impossible to make them conceive the one without the other Christianity is the companion of liberty in all its conflicts — the cradle of its infancy, and the divine source of its claims.

What a great role fervent preaching has played in America's past, and what great importance there is to keep it continuing in the present, guiding us into the ways of liberty and true prosperity.

THE FAITH OF OUR FATHERS
Their Beliefs in the Bible, Prayer, & Christianity

After our founding fathers declared their independence and fought for eight years and six months, they won that independence against insurmountable odds. However, their initial "constitution" was the Articles of Confederation. After twelve years of government under it, things did not seem to be working as expected. The Articles of Confederation was weak in its power. It allowed the states to carry on more individually than united as one nation with one central government. Some of its strong points were that it allowed Congress to raise armies, to declare war, and to sign treaties; but, it did not allow Congress to raise revenue through taxes or regulate trade and collect tariffs. This resulted in much "division" and "individualism" in the colonies. Each of the thirteen different colonies...acted more as if there were thirteen different "countries," thirteen different currencies, thirteen different foreign policies, thirteen different tariffs, and more.

With our government "spinning its wheels," financially broke and with its hands tied, with invasion and compromise imminent – our founding fathers joined together once again in the same place where they had come together to ascribe to the Declaration of Independence. They gathered to see if they could form a more perfect union. The time had come. The need was very great. Great Britain still had troops stationed to the north, and two of the thirteen states were ready to sign treaties with their former tyrant if nothing availed. France and Spain were to the south, ready to invade if this "Experiment in Liberty" was to fall apart.

They met for five and a half weeks, they debated, and they could agree on absolutely *nothing*. Fifty percent of the people lived in three states and the other fifty percent of the people lived in ten states, and there was no way around things. Five states said, *"We don't want to abolish slavery."* Eight states said, *"Hey, we didn't fight for freedom to have slavery continue."* And there was an impasse. In the midst of one of the heated arguments, along with other delegates, George Mason, George Washington's good friend and neighbor, stood up and walked out. Mason originally had stated at the beginning of the convention that he would rather bury his bones in Philadelphia than quit with no solution found. However, the debates were slow-moving and discouraging with nothing being achieved. Washington, being a humble man, compassionately stood and walked out with him bringing his arm to his friend's shoulder. Underneath the sunny sky on the front steps the Independence Hall, Washington pleaded with him. *"Please don't leave... We have a nation to form."* But George Mason, along with many other people said, *"We have better things to do than to just sit in there and argue!"* However, they were convinced to stay for just a little while longer and to give it one more chance.

On June 28, 1787, our Founding Fathers were facing an awful and critical moment at the convention. There was a serious impasse between the flustered delegates each with their own heated opinions. Georgia representative William Few described, *"If the Convention had then adjourned, the dissolution of the union of the states seemed inevitable."*

In the midst of these great difficulties, Dr. Ben Franklin – one of six of the original fifty-six signers of the Declaration of Independence who had made it back to sign the Constitution – now in his eighties and ill, arose and walked down to the front of the assembly, heavily leaving upon his cane. With thick silence hanging in the air as each man waited for his words, he delivered from his heart the following address:

"The small progress we have made after four or five weeks, is proof of the imperfection of human understanding. We have gone back to ancient history for models of government and examined the different forms which now no longer

exist. We have viewed modern states all around Europe but find none of their constitutions suitable to our circumstances. In this situation, groping in the dark to find political truth...have we not once thought of humbly applying to the Father of Lights to illuminate our understanding?"

Eyes began to squint in thought. Hearts began to soften. Eyes began to moisten. Stubbornness would soon give way to submission as Franklin continued – taking all of them back into recent dark times, *"In the beginning of the contest with Great Britain, when we were sensible of danger, we had daily prayer in this room for Divine protection."*

Think about what he is saying. In the beginning, in Independence Hall, in Philadelphia – Franklin had been there in 1776, almost a decade earlier. He had been there when their backs were "up against the wall" and they did not know where to turn except for looking up to God and pleading for help and assistance in His Divine Providence. Men in the room began to realize this. They understood. Heads began to lower. Men looked down to the floor or gazed past Franklin deep in thought, realizing that God had been there for them and with them... understanding now that they had not even acknowledged Him.

Franklin continued, snapping men out of their thoughts, *"Our prayers were heard, and they were graciously answered. All of us engaged in the struggle must have observed frequent instances of Superintending Providence in our favor. And have we now forgotten this Powerful Friend? Or do we imagine we no longer need His assistance? I have lived...a long time, and the longer I live, the more convincing proofs I see of this truth – that God governs the affairs of men. If a sparrow cannot fall to the ground without His notice, is it probable that an empire can rise without His aid? We have been assured in the Sacred Writings that 'Except the Lord build the house, they labor in vain that build it.' I firmly believe this; and I also believe without His concurring aid we shall succeed in this political building no better than the builders of Babel. I therefore beg leave to move that, henceforth, prayers imploring the assistance of Heaven and its blessing on our deliberation be held in this assembly every morning before we proceed to business."*

As Benjamin Franklin sat down, Representative Jonathan Dayton of New Jersey relates that he never saw *"a countenance...so dignified and delighted as was that of Washington at the close of the address; nor were the members of the convention generally less affected. The words of the venerable Franklin fell upon ears with a weight and authority...."*

James Madison moved, seconded by Roger Sherman of Connecticut, that Franklin's appeal for prayer be enacted. Though the challenge was well received and highly favored by the delegates, some were afraid that the convention would not have enough money to pay a preacher to come in and pray daily. Others were fearful that such news of "outside" ministers coming in to conduct prayer time and devotions would start rumors throughout the states that chaos and disharmony were breaking out in the Constitutional convention. Men were beginning to become hesitant to go through with this noble yet necessary course of action.

In the midst of the quietly exchanged words of concern, Edmund Jennings Randolph of Virginia stood and recommended: *"That a sermon be preached at the request of the convention on the 4th of July, the anniversary of Independence; & thenceforward prayers be used in ye Convention every morning."* Ben Franklin himself eagerly seconded this motion and soon after the excited delegates favorably voted upon it. And with that, they recessed. Many men were smitten in their hearts with conviction and slowly, quietly filed out of Independence Hall. Most Americans unfortunately do not realize that many of the delegates got alone with God for the next three days, either in churches or in their private quarters, and prayed and fasted, begging Jehovah God for forgiveness and Holy Spirit wisdom.

They then reconvened, and every day for the next five weeks they prayed and asked God for His guidance and discernment in the formulation of our Constitution. Jonathan Dayton recorded that when they assembled again, every *"unfriendly feeling had been expelled, and a spirit of conciliation had been cultivated."* On July 4th, the entire assembly of delegates gathered and worshipped together at the Reformed Calvinistic Lutheran Church in Philadelphia, sincerely asking God with one voice and heart for Him to guide them in the formulation of America's new and necessary Constitution.

Alexander Hamilton reflected years later, looking back on the proceedings of the Constitutional Convention, *"For my own part, I sincerely esteem it a system which without the finger of God, never could have been suggested and agreed upon by such a diversity of interests."*

James Madison declared, *"It is impossible for any man of candor to reflect on this circumstance without partaking of the astonishment. It is impossible for the man of pious reflection not to perceive in it a finger of that Almighty hand which has been so frequently and signally extended to our relief in the critical stages of the revolution."*

Our Constitution is the most miraculous of all governmental documents, because it has given us, the United States of America, all the opportunities, all the abundance, and all the liberties that we share.

Our founders also determined, *"Let us recognize from where our wisdom comes,"* setting a precedent of prayer before each assembly. Therefore, Congress has never met in the history of the United States without going to prayer. That means every time Congress has met, even if it met for five minutes, they have prayed to Almighty God. Our founders also said, *"We shall put on our currency, it is in God whom we will put our trust."* **IN GOD WE TRUST.** That is the true motto of this country, because we recognize as a nation that our dependency is upon Him.

Every other government and constitution has changed since that time. Our Constitution has continued as a template and the apex in human government...because it is based upon God, prayer, and the Bible – article upon article. Every year that passes in this nation, we celebrate and set a new record of God-given freedoms that we can wonderfully enjoy.

It cannot be emphasized or repeated enough: this is all because our forefathers had a deep faith and trust in God. This is the reason for our greatness. We have been a people of faith. We have recognized our Creator from the earliest days. This faith in God and God's Word has influenced our Constitution, our laws, and has shaped our national conscience for over 230 years. We were formed without apology as a "Christian nation" by those who did not want a state religion or state church, but wanted a nation guided by the truths of Christianity. It is truly amazing how our forefathers recognized and loved God and implored Him to bless, guide, and protect this nation.

Let us take a few moments and consider in their own words, the faith and beliefs of our forefathers and other great Americans throughout our history concerning the Bible, prayer, and the importance of Christianity.

THE BIBLE

"It is impossible to rightly govern the world without God and the Bible." – **George Washington, 1752**

"This is the Book. I have read the Bible through many times, and now make it a practice to read it through once every year… It is a book of all others for lawyers, as well as divines; and I pity the man who cannot find in it a rich supply of thought and of rules for conduct. It fits man for life – it prepares him for death." – **Daniel Webster, 1843**

"The Bible is the Chief moral cause of all that is good, and the best corrector of all that is evil, in human society; the best book for regulating the temporal concerns of men, and the only book that can serve as an infallible guide to future felicity… It is extremely important to our nation, in a political as well as religious view, that all possible authority and influence should be given to the Scriptures, for these furnish the best principles of civil liberty, and the most effectual support of republican government. The principles of genuine liberty, and of wise laws and administrations, are to be drawn from the Bible and sustained by its authority. The man, therefore, who weakens or destroys the divine authority of that Book may be accessory to all the public disorders which society is doomed to suffer…." – **Noah Webster, 1833**

"Hold fast to the Bible as the sheet anchor of your liberties; write its precepts in your hearts, and practice them in your lives. To the influence of this Book are we indebted for all the progress made in true civilization, and to this must we look as our guide in the future." – **President Ulysses S. Grant, 1876**

"The Bible is the cornerstone of liberty." – **President Thomas Jefferson**

"The greatest enemy of the salvation of man, never invented a more effectual means of extirpating Christianity from the world than by persuading mankind that it was improper to read the Bible at schools." – **Benjamin Rush, 1789**

"All societies of men must be governed in some way or other. Men, in a word, must necessarily be controlled either by a power within them, or a power without them; either by the Word of God, or by the strong arm of man; either by the Bible or by the bayonet." – **John Winthrop, 1849**

"The moral principles and precepts contained in the Scriptures ought to form the basis of all of our civil constitutions and laws. All the miseries and evils which men suffer from vice, crime, ambition, injustice, oppression, slavery, and war, proceed from their despising or neglecting the precepts contained in the Bible." – **Noah Webster, 1829**

"The laws of the Christian system, as embraced by the Bible, must be respected as of high authority in all our courts and it cannot be thought improper for the officers of such government to acknowledge their obligation to govern by its rule. Our government originating in the voluntary compact of a people who in that very instrument profess the Christian religion, it may be considered, not a republic like Rome was, a Pagan but a Christian republic." – **Nathaniel Freeman, 1802**

"The first and almost the only Book deserving of universal attention is the Bible. I speak as a man of the world to men of the world; and I say to you, Search the Scriptures! The Bible is the book of all others, to be read at all ages, and in all conditions of human life; not to be read once or twice or thrice through, and then laid aside, but to be read in small portions of one or two chapters every day. In what light soever we regard the Bible, it is an invaluable and inexhaustible mine of knowledge and virtue." – **John Quincy Adams, 6th President of the United States**

"I believe the Bible is the best gift God has given to man. All the good Saviour gave to the world was communicated through this Book. But for this Book we could not know right from wrong. All things most desirable for man's welfare… are to be found portrayed in it." – **Abraham Lincoln, 16th President of the United States**

"I have examined all religions my busy life would allow; and the result is that the Bible is the best Book in the world. It contains more philosophy than all the libraries I have seen." – **John Adams, 2nd President of the United States**

"If we abide by the principles taught in the Bible, our country will go on prospering and to prosper; If we and our posterity shall be true to the Christian religion, if we and they shall live always in the fear of God and shall respect His commandments, we may have the highest hopes of the future fortunes of our country. But if we and our posterity neglect religious instruction and authority; violate the rules of eternal justice, trifle with the injunctions of morality, and recklessly destroy the political constitution which holds us together, no man can tell how sudden a catastrophe may overwhelm us and bury all our glory in profound obscurity." – **Daniel Webster**

"We have staked the whole future of American civilization, not upon the power of government, far from it. We have staked the future ... upon the capacity of each and all of us to govern ourselves, to sustain ourselves, according to the Ten Commandments of God." – **President James Madison**

"The purpose of a devout and united people was set forth in the pages of The Bible... (1) to live in freedom, (2) to work in a prosperous land...and (3) to obey the commandments of God....This Biblical story of the Promised land inspired the founders of America. It continues to inspire us...." – **President Dwight D. Eisenhower**

"The right to freedom being the gift of God Almighty...the rights of the Colonists as Christians...may best be understood by reading and carefully studying the institutions of The Great Law Giver and the Head of the Christian Church, which are to be found clearly written and promulgated in the New Testament." – **Samuel Adams**

"If American democracy is to remain the greatest hope of humanity, it must continue abundantly in the faith of the Bible" – **President Calvin Coolidge**

"The Bible is the rock on which our Republic rests." – **President Andrew Jackson**

PRAYER

"I conceive that we cannot better express ourselves than by humbly supplicating the Supreme Ruler of the world that the role of tyrants may be broken to pieces, and the oppressed made free again." – **Samuel Adams**

"I yield Thee humble and hearty thanks, that Thou hast preserved me from the dangers of the night past and brought me to the light of this day. Let my heart therefore Gracious God be so affected with the glory and majesty of it, that I may not do mine own works but wait on Thee, and since Thou are a God of pure eyes, and will be sanctified in all who draw nearer to Thee, who dost not regard the sacrifice of fools, nor hear sinners who tread in Thy courts, pardon I beseech Thee, my sins, remove them from Thy presence, as far as the east is from the west, and accept me for the merits of Thy Son Jesus Christ." – **George Washington, 1ˢᵗ President of the United States**

"Remember ever, and always, that your country was founded, not by the 'most superficial, the lightest, the most irreflective of all European races,' but by the [Pilgrims] who made the deck of the Mayflower an altar of the living God, and whose first act on touching the soil of the new world was to offer on bended knees thanksgiving to Almighty God." – **Henry Wilson**

"I have been driven many times upon my knees by the overwhelming conviction that I had nowhere else to go. My own wisdom, and that of all about me, seem insufficient for that day." – **Abraham Lincoln**

"Almighty God, Who has given us this good land for our heritage; We humbly beseech Thee that we may always prove ourselves a people mindful of Thy favor and glad to do Thy will. Bless our land with honorable ministry, sound learning, and pure manners. Save us from violence, discord, and confusion, from pride and arrogance, and from every evil way. Defend our liberties, and fashion into one united people the multitude brought hither out of many kindreds and tongues. Endow with Thy spirit of wisdom those to whom in Thy Name we entrust the authority of government, that there may be justice and peace at home, and that through obedience to Thy law, we may show forth Thy praise among the nations of the earth. In time of prosperity fill our hearts with thankfulness, and in

the day of trouble, suffer not our trust in Thee to fail; all of which we ask through Jesus Christ our Lord, Amen." – **President Thomas Jefferson, 1805**

"Knowing that intercessory prayer is our mightiest weapon and the supreme call for all Christians today, I pleadingly urge our people everywhere to pray. Believing that prayer is the greatest contribution that our people can make in this critical hour, I humbly urge that we take time to pray – to really pray. Let there be prayer at sunup, at noon-day, at sundown, at midnight – all through the day. Let us pray for our children, our youth, our aged, our pastors, our homes. Let us pray for our churches. Let us pray for ourselves, that we may not lose the word 'concern' out of our Christian vocabulary. Let us pray for our nation. Let us pray for those who have never known Jesus Christ and redeeming love, for moral forces everywhere, for our national leaders. Let prayer be our passion. Let prayer be our practice." – **Robert E. Lee**

"Direct my thoughts, words and work, wash away my sins in the immaculate Blood of the Lamb, and purge my heart by Thy Holy Spirit, from the dross of my natural corruption, that I may with more freedom of mind and liberty of will serve Thee, the Everlasting God, in righteousness and holiness this day, and all the days of my life. Increase my faith in the sweet promises of the Gospel; give me repentance from dead works; pardon my wanderings, and direct my thoughts unto Thyself, the God of my salvation; teach me how to live in Thy fear, labor in Thy service, and ever to run in the ways of Thy commandments; make me always watchful over my heart, that neither the terrors of conscience, the loathing of holy duties, the love of sin, nor the unwillingness to depart this life, may cast me into a spiritual slumber, but daily frame me more and more into the likeness of Thy Son, Jesus Christ, that living in Thy fear, and dying in Thy favor, I may in Thy appointed time attain the resurrection of the just unto eternal life." – **President George Washington**

IMPORTANCE OF CHRISTIANITY

"It is my conviction that our government rests on religion; that religion is the source from which we derive our reverence for truth and justice, for equality and liberty, and for the rights of mankind. If the bonds of our religious convictions become loosened the guaranties which have been erected for the protection of life

and liberty and all the vast body of rights that lies between, are gone. America was born in a revival of religion." – **Calvin Coolidge, 30th President of the United States**

"If thou wouldst rule well, thou must rule for God, and to do that, thou must be ruled by Him. Those who will not be governed by God will be ruled by tyrants." – **William Penn, founder of Pennsylvania**

"First, the doctrines of Jesus are simple and tend to the happiness of man. Second, there is only one God, and He is all perfect. Third, there is a future state of rewards and punishment. Four, to love God with all the heart and thy neighbor as thyself is the sum of all. Had there never been a commentator there never would have been an infidel. I have little doubt that the whole country will soon be rallied to the unity of our Creator, and, I hope, to the pure doctrines of Jesus also. If a nation expects to be ignorant and free, in a state of civilization, it expects what never was and never will be. Among the most inestimable of our blessings is that…of liberty to worship our Creator in the way we think most agreeable in His will; a liberty deemed in other countries incompatible with good government and yet proved by our experience to be its best support." – **Thomas Jefferson, 3rd President of the United States**

"Christianity is the only true and perfect religion, and that in proportion as mankind adopts its principles and obeys its precepts, they will be wise and happy." – **Benjamin Rush, 1798**

"No nation has ever yet existed or been governed without religion. Nor can be. The Christian religion is the best religion that has ever been given to man and I as chief Magistrate of this nation am bound to give it the sanction of my example." – **Thomas Jefferson**

"Religion is the solid basis of good morals; therefore education should teach the precepts of religion, and the duties of man toward God." – **Gouverneur Morris**

"…Those nations only are blessed whose God is the Lord." – **President Abraham Lincoln**

"Finally, let us not forget the religious character of our origin. Our fathers were brought hither by their high veneration for the Christian religion. They journeyed by its light, and labored in its hope. They sought to incorporate its principles with the elements of their society, and to diffuse its influence through all their institutions, civil, political, or literary." – **Daniel Webster**

"Where there is no religion, there is no morality…. With the loss of religion…the ultimate foundation of confidence is blown up; and the security of life, liberty, and property are buried in ruins." – **Timothy Dwight, President of Yale College, 1798**

"Without religion, I believe that learning does real mischief to the morals and principles of mankind." – **Benjamin Rush**

"Under God's Power She Flourishes." – **Princeton University's official motto**

"You do well to wish to learn our arts and ways of life, and above all, the religion of Jesus Christ." – **George Washington to the Delaware Indian chiefs**

"The land we possesses is the gift of heaven to our fathers and Divine Providence seems to have decreed it to our latest posterity." – **William Livingston**

"…True religion affords to government its surest support." – **President George Washington**

"It is not the talking but the walking and the working person that is the true Christian." – **President James Madison**

"Neither the wisest constitution nor the wisest laws will secure the liberty and happiness of a people whose manners are universally corrupt." – **Samuel Adams**

"We have no King but Jesus!" – **a rallying cry for American independence from the tyranny of England**

"Of all the dispositions and habits which lead to political prosperity, religion and morality are indispensable supports. In vain would that man claim the tribute of patriotism, who should labor to subvert these great pillars of human happiness.... And let us with caution indulge the supposition that morality can be maintained without religion." – **President George Washington**

"The religion, which has introduced civil liberty, is the religion of Christ and His apostles, which enjoins humility, piety, and benevolence; which acknowledges in every person a brother, or a sister, and a citizen with equal rights. This is genuine Christianity, and to this we owe our free Constitutions of government." – **Noah Webster, 1832**

"Whenever the pillars of Christianity shall be overthrown, our present republican forms of government, and all the blessings which flow from them, must fall with them." – **Jedediah Morse, 1799**

"America was born a Christian nation. America was born to exemplify that devotion to the elements of righteousness, which are derived from the revelations of Holy Scripture." – **President Woodrow Wilson, 1911**

"It cannot be emphasized too strongly or too often that this great nation was founded, not by religionists, but by Christians; not on religions, but on the Gospel of Jesus Christ. For this very reason peoples of other faiths have been afforded asylum, prosperity, and freedom of worship here." – **Patrick Henry**

John Quincy Adams said, *"The United States of America were no longer Colonies [after the War for Independence]. They were an independent nation of Christians."* Roughly 97% of the Founding Fathers were practicing Christians and exercised their faith in public office, at work, at home, and had it taught to their children in their schools. We must remember that the Bible was the chief textbook in the public school, and children learned it well. Every one of our Founding Fathers received a Christian education based on the Bible. Furthermore, over 40% of the signers of the Declaration of Independence had seminary degrees.

Several signers of the Constitution founded Bible societies and publicly practiced their Christian faith. Charles Pinckney and John Langdon were founders of the American Bible Society. James McHenry was a founder of the Baltimore Bible Society. Rufus King helped found a Bible society for Anglicans. Abraham Baldwin was renowned for his piety and devotion to his duties as a chaplain in the army during the War of Independence. James Wilson and William Paterson had prayer over juries as U. S. Supreme Court Justices. Roger Sherman, William Samuel Johnson, John Dickinson, and Jacob Broom were Christian theological authors.

In December, 1982, the *Newsweek* Magazine shocked America – both liberals and conservatives – with the remarkable truth revealing to us the importance of the Bible and the faith of the Founding Fathers in our past: *"For centuries the Bible has exerted an unrivaled influence on American culture, politics, and social life. Now historians are discovering that the Bible, perhaps even more than the Constitution, is our founding document: the source of the powerful myth of the United States as a special, sacred nation, a people called by God to establish a model society, a beacon to the world."*

Even the least "religious" of our Founding Fathers, such as Benjamin Franklin and Thomas Jefferson, were regular Bible readers and had an understanding of it. The personal and political writings of our forefathers were heavily sprinkled with Scriptural quotations and illustrations. **At least 50 out of the 55 men who framed the Constitution of the United States were professing Christians**, since eleven of the first thirteen States required faith in Jesus Christ and in the Bible qualifications for holding public office.

According to the massive research conducted by Donald Lutz and Charles Hyneman, after examining 15,000 documents, books, and political writings by our Founding Fathers from 1760-1805, 34% of the 3,154 quotations referencing other sources came from the Bible. Our Founding Fathers quoted the Bible four times more than other source or individual. In addition, the other sources they most frequently quoted were written by men who were professing Christians and whose views on government, politics, and law were directly influenced by God's Word.

Without a doubt, the Bible and prayer were key elements in the founding of America. Our Forefathers believed in the authority of God's Word, and they depended upon the guidance of the Divine Providence to illuminate their understanding in order to establish a nation flourishing with Biblical prosperity. This is our true American heritage!

CHAPTER V

UNDER GOD?
The Current Crisis of American Education

On June 14, 1954, President Dwight Eisenhower supported and signed into law the Congressional Act, Joint Resolution 243, which added the phrase "under God" to our *Pledge of Allegiance*. Our *Pledge* was originally written by Francis Bellamy, a Baptist preacher from Boston, who was also on staff at *The Youth's Companion* Magazine which published this pledge on September 8, 1892. On October 12, at the dedication of the 1892 Chicago World's Fair, public school children first recited this *Pledge of Allegiance* during the National School Celebration on the 400th anniversary of Columbus' discovery of America. The words "under God" were taken from President Abraham Lincoln's famous Gettysburg Address, in which he stated *"…that this nation, under God, shall have a new birth of freedom – and that government of the people, by the people, for the people, shall not perish from the earth."* With this in mind, President Eisenhower declared, *"In this way we are reaffirming the transcendence of religious faith in America's heritage and future; in this way we shall constantly strengthen those spiritual weapons which forever will be our country's most powerful resource in peace and war."* And upon the steps of the U.S. Capitol he recited the *Pledge of Allegiance* with the phrase "one nation under God" for the first time. President Eisenhower reflected, *"From this day forward, the millions of our school children will daily proclaim in every city and town, every village and rural school house, the dedication of our nation and our people to the Almighty. To anyone who truly loves America, nothing could be more inspiring than to contemplate this rededication of our youth, on each school morning, to our country's truest meaning."*

Less than 10 years later in 1963 – prayer, the Bible, and the reading of it were banned from our public schools...and there has been a movement in this country to remove those sacred words "under God" from our *Pledge of Allegiance.*

Madalyn Murray O' Hair, a Marxist and atheist, wickedly desired to remove all expressions of Christianity, Bible-reading, and prayer from the public school system. In her lawsuit *Murray v. Curlett* she filed with the Supreme Court in 1963, she used her teenage son, William J. Murray, to protest daily Bible reading, the recitation of the Lord's Prayer, and other prayers in the Baltimore Public Schools.

In the decisions rendered on June 25, 1962, in *Engel v. Vitale,* and on June 17, 1963, in *Murray v. Curlett* and *Abington v. Schempp,* the Supreme Court forbade any religious activities in the students' daily lives at American public schools, declaring that it was unconstitutional. When the Bible – society's only true standard of absolute truth and morality – God, and prayer were banned, a great ideological shift began. Catastrophe would soon commence.

The prayer the court objected to specifically was, *"Almighty God, we acknowledge our dependence upon Thee, and we beg Thy blessings upon us, our parents, our teachers, and our country."* God had been honoring that prayer. At that time, the public school system was the most excellent educational system in the world and SAT scores were the highest ever. Now, SAT test scores on average have gone down 80 points. International comparisons of student achievement reveal that on nineteen academic tests, American students were never first or second and were last seven times. In a test comparing average American public school sixth graders with their counterparts in seven other Western industrialized countries, American public school students ranked last in mathematics and not much better in science and geography. Fourteen-year-old science students placed fourteenth out of seventeen competing countries. Advanced American science students were ninth out of the thirteen countries in physics, eleventh of thirteen in chemistry, and last in biology. At the turn of the 21st century, an estimated 90 million people were functionally illiterate and 26% of all 17 year olds failed to graduate from high school. In 1993, approximately 700,000 students who graduated could not read their own diploma and many of those who could read have difficulty with comprehension. By the mid-1990's, about one in every five Americans read below the fourth-grade level.

Before God, the Bible, and prayer were banned, the top public school problems were simply: talking out of turn, chewing gum in class, making unnecessary noise in class or study hall, running in the hallways, getting out of turn in line, wearing improper clothing, and not throwing paper into the waste basket. **After** God, the Bible, and prayer were removed, our morality and academics seriously declined; and, crimes, rebellion, and illiteracy crazily increased. Words of respect, kindness, and innocent jest are replaced with profanity, vile language, a "you-can't-make-me" attitude, and fights in the hallways…starting from the ages of 5 and up! (Ann Landers, cited in Schools in Crisis, page 6) According to the *USA Today* in September, 1985, roughly twenty years later, the top offenses at public schools were drastically different: rape, robbery, assault, burglary, arson, absenteeism, vandalism, drug abuse, alcohol abuse, gang warfare, pregnancies, abortions, and venereal disease.

Since that time, violent crimes have risen 995%, premarital sex for 15 year olds has risen 1000%, premarital sex for 16-18 year olds has risen 300%, suicides have risen 300%, single parent families have risen 117%, unwed teen pregnancies have risen 553% for 15 year olds and 300% for 16-18 year olds, unmarried couples living together has risen 536%, sexually transmitted diseases have risen 226%, divorce has risen 117%, child abuse has risen 2,300%, illegal drug use has risen 6,000%, crimes against fellow students have risen 3,000%, and assaults on teachers have risen 7,000%. There are 100 murders; 12,000 robberies; 9,000 rapes; and 204,000 aggressive assaults on school campuses annually.

As Americans, we must realize that from the very beginning of our history, the Bible was the chief textbook in the public school, and children learned it well. Children learned not only to be good, but also why they should be good. A respect for the Bible was instilled in children at a young age, and as a result, the standard of morality found in that Book was held by most as a way of life. By the turn of the 19th century, President John Adams stated that finding an illiterate man in New England was as rare as finding a comet in the night sky.

Significantly, America's first public education law, "The Ol' Deluder Satan Act", was passed in 1647 to prevent *"that old deluder, Satan, to keep men from the knowledge of the Scriptures."* Virtually all the colonists – both frontiersmen and our Founding Fathers – received a thorough Christian education from elementary school to college.

America's first textbook, *The New England Primer*, heavily relied upon the Bible and was used in American classrooms until the 1930's. As a young colonist child learned each letter of his alphabet in the *New England Primer*, he would learn a Bible principle to go along with it:

A	**B**	**C**
In ADAM'S Fall	*Heaven to find;*	*Christ crucify'd*
We sinned all.	*The Bible Mind.*	*For sinners dy'd*

In older grades, he was taught to read using magnificent truths based on the Word of God, NOT "Jane and Spot" or some other basic child's book.

A wise son maketh a glad father, but a foolish son is the heaviness of his mother.

Better is a little with the fear of the Lord, than great treasure and trouble therewith.

Come unto Christ all ye that labor and are heavy laden and he will give you rest.

Consider one of the lessons from the *New England Primer* entitled "A Lesson for Children":

Pray to God.	*Call no ill names.*
Love God.	*Use no ill words.*
Fear God.	*Tell no lies.*
Serve God.	*Hate lies.*
Take not God's	*Speak the Truth.*
Name in Vain.	*Spend your Time well.*
Do not Swear.	*Love your School.*
Do not Steal.	*Mind your Book.*
Cheat not in your play.	*Strive to learn.*
Play not with bad boys.	*Be not a Dunce.*

The colleges in the first thirteen states of America were greatly influenced by the Word of God during the colonial period, and many were originally established with the main purpose of training men for the ministry of Jesus Christ, either filling the colonies' pulpits with zealous preachers or preparing others, like David Brainerd, for missions work to the Indians in the wilderness. In fact, 106 of the first 108 universities in America were Christian colleges. Now they have turned into godless, atheistic Ivy League schools. Consider one of the requirements for Yale college students during the 1700's: *"Seeing that God is the giver of all wisdom, every scholar, besides private or secret prayer… shall be present morning and evening at public prayer."*

The first English-language Bible printed in America was in 1782, printed by the Continental Congress as *"a neat edition of the Holy Scriptures for the use of our schools."* In 1789, Congress passed the first federal law addressing education, requiring that schools teach *"religion, morality, and knowledge."* In 1791, Benjamin Rush, a signer of the Declaration of Independence, wrote a policy pamphlet setting forth a dozen reasons why the Bible should never be taken out of the schools. He said, *"We profess to be republicans, and yet we neglect the only means of establishing and perpetuating our republican forms of government; that is, the universal education of our youth in the principles of Christianity by means of the Bible; for this divine book, above all others, favors that equality among mankind, that respect for just laws, and all those sober and frugal virtues which constitute the soul of republicanism."*

While Thomas Jefferson was President of the United States, he also was the District of Colombia's school board chairman. He wrote its first "plan of education" that they used for many years. This called for the Bible and Isaac Watts' *Psalms, Hymns, and Spiritual Songs* to be used as the primary textbooks for reading assignments and teaching the students how to read.

In 1844, an unanimous United States Supreme Court declared: *"Why may not the Bible, and especially the New Testament...be read and taught as a divine revelation in school? Where can the purest principles of morality be learned so clearly or so perfectly as from the New Testament?"* There are dozens of similar examples, and this remained the standard until 1962-1963, when the U.S. Supreme Court first ordered the removal of voluntary prayer and Bible reading from public education.

President George Washington, in his Farewell Address, stated, *"And let us with caution indulge the supposition that morality can be maintained without religion... reason and experience forbid us to expect that national morality can prevail in exclusion of religious principle."*

David Barton declares: *"School prayer was the simplest identification of a philosophy recognizing not only the God of heaven, but also His laws and standards of conduct as well. For example, where prayer is found, it is not surprising also to find the Bible, the Ten Commandments, and traditional moral teachings, etc. Conversely, where there is an absence of prayer, it is not surprising that there is also an absence of biblical principles or traditional values. In fact, it would be surprising to find religious values present where prayer is absent."* (*America: To Pray or Not to Pray?*, page 32)

Martin Luther warned future generations over half a millennia ago, *"...I am very much afraid that schools will prove to be the great gates of hell unless they diligently labor in explaining the Holy Scriptures...engraving them in the hearts of the youth. I advise no one to place his child where the Scriptures do not reign paramount. Every institution in which men are not increasingly occupied with the Word of God must become corrupt."*

Abraham Lincoln recognized that *"The philosophy of the classroom in this generation will be the philosophy of politics, government, and life in the next."* Consider his words of wisdom as we peer into the truth of what American youth are learning in the classroom today.

It seems that the public school system could care less that they have lost considerable ground academically over the years, but focuses more on continuing with their agenda to brainwash American youth with humanism, socialism, multiculturalism, blatant paganism, and New Age philosophy.

Now that Bible-reading and prayer are "illegal" in the public school, the godless liberals and atheists who run these schools are eager to enforce the ban. Dr. David C. Gibbs, Jr., the president of the Christian Law Association, in his book *One Nation Under God*, reveals that Christian public school students have been threatened with being expelled if they talked about Jesus in the classroom. One student failed a test because he refused to answer a question asking students to prove the scientific falsity of the Biblical claim that Moses parted the Red Sea; public school officials planned to place one of their students in detention because she brought her Bible to school; another was told that she could not place a Ten Commandments poster on her locker even though other students were allowed to put whatever secular poster they wanted on their lockers. Another young man was told that he could not read his Bible, Christian magazines, or a book about the Constitution and Christian principles during his public school independent reading time. This is just a few of the many infringements upon our liberties in the public school system, showing how far we have drifted from the mindset and hearts' desire of our founding fathers!

Over 400 billion dollars are spent every year on the education of our youth, yet what are they learning? Instead of children knowing how to effectively read and write by Kindergarten or first grade as they should, they are learning it by the fourth grade. *How is that possible?* It is time that we as Americans and as Christian recognize the truth about the public school system!

In all reality, children are learning that God is irrelevant, possibly a "Higher Power," and that billions of years ago there was a big BANG and here we are. Children are learning that the Bible is an outdated "manual" of fairy tales teaching people to hate, that the toleration of bad things is actually a virtue and is a wonderful quality of character, that vocalizing morality is a hate crime, and that Bible-believing Christians are fanatics. America's youth are learning that big business, with the help of Republican presidents, are ruining our environment. They are learning that our Founding Fathers were racists, atheists, and revolutionaries who should be identified with Karl Marx (the Father of Communism who said, *"My objective in life is to dethrone God and destroy capitalism"*). They are taught that the Alamo was a great Mexican victory; that society rather than the individual is responsible for crime; that the Constitution is obsolete; that saving the white spotted owl is more important than saving the unborn child; that homosexuality is just one of many different acceptable alternative life-styles; and that the First Amendment of our Constitution requires the government to censor religious speech, but every other ungodly form of communication is to be tolerated as "free speech." (Interestingly, in 1798, Thomas Jefferson wrote that *"no power over the freedom of religion...[is] delegated to the United States by the Constitution."*) Our children are learning that it is the government's responsibility is to provide jobs, housing, clothing, hot lunches, living wages, retirement, and healthcare to all of its citizens; that loyalty to a global world order is far more important than loyalty to the United States of America; and that loyalty to the President is more vital than loyalty to the Constitution. Where have we gone as a nation? How far we have drifted from the truth!

Modern textbooks are undermining the values and authority of parents by using a form of reasoning called "values clarification" – a program that encourages children to doubt, distrust, and eventually deny the moral, ethical, and Biblical values they were taught. Here is an excerpt from a classroom textbook: *"A major influence on you has been the attitudes and behaviors of each of your parents...You have probably learned some fairly traditional ideas...Many people believe these traditional attitudes hinder growth and development of a person because they limit possibilities...Only you can judge."* (Evans, Pearl, Hidden Danger in the Classroom, Small Helm Press, page 49)

Chester M. Pierce, M.D., Professor of Education and Psychiatry at Harvard University compelled public school teachers:

"Every child in America entering school at the age five is mentally ill because he comes to school with certain allegiances to our Founding Fathers, toward our elected officials, toward his parents, toward a belief in a supernatural being, and toward the sovereignty of this nation as a separate entity. It's up to you as teachers to make all these sick children well – by creating the international child of the future."

In public schools, young people are forced to learn "sex education." At young ages children are learning about this wonderful act that God ordained for only within the boundaries of marriage as if it was a flippant thing that needs to be practiced until they are good at it. Professor Donn Byrne of Psychological Sciences at Purdue University and chairman of the Social-Personality Program wickedly stated: *"But in order to free students from religious hang-ups, sex educators must rid them of their feelings of guilt and anxiety about natural sexual functions."* By fifth grade, children are encourage to participate in this activity in some way or another. Author Carl Sommers declares, *"There are two ways to destroy a society: by overcoming it from without by the use of superior military might, or by overpowering it from within by encouraging such forces as will foster internal moral decay."*

The next barrage of wicked indoctrination in the public school system that is rapidly spreading throughout America is children learning to tolerate homosexuality. They are taught that it is completely ordinary, and to have homosexual desires is completely normal and healthy. Second through fifth graders will gather in assembly at their elementary schools and learn slogans like "I'm gay and it's OK." They will be exposed to the fact that there are all kinds of families today including those who have two mommies or two daddies. They will watch various skits about it – including one in which Rapunzel cuts off her hair and runs away with her girlfriend to live happily ever after. These assemblies are conducted by groups such as *Cootie Shots*, which branched off from and is funded by the Gay, Lesbian, and Straight Education Network. The GLSEN states that *"It is imperative to begin addressing these issues in the elementary schools as early as possible."* Children and teenagers are being provided with "hot line" phone numbers that will offer homosexual sensitive counseling. Elementary, junior high, and high schools are being flooded with literature, videos, and testimonials advocating the pro-gay perspective, encouraging students to explore and embrace their homosexual desires.

In "The Overhauling of Straight America," an article published in a 1987 *Guide* magazine, the sodomites revealed a preview of their plan: *"The first order of business is desensitization of the American public concerning gays and gay rights. To desensitize the public is to help it view homosexuality with indifference instead of with keen emotion."*

Then in 2001, the mainstream gay activist groups in California assembled and planned how to thoroughly penetrate the public school system, to gain more recruits to their lifestyles, and to desensitize the minds of the youth through tolerance and acceptance. These goals included:

- *Surveying children to probe their attitudes about homosexuality.*
- *Integrating pro-homosexual and pro-transgender messages into "all" curricula, including science, history, language, arts, and even math*
- *Creating new policies "to reduce the adverse impact of gender segregation…related to locker room facilities, restrooms, and dress."*
- *Posting "positive grade level appropriate visual images" that included "all sexual orientations and gender identities" throughout the school.*
- *Using taxpayer dollars to establish Gay-Straight Alliances on campuses, put all school personnel through extensive and "ongoing" sensitivity training, pay for a media blitz, "provide rehabilitation to perpetrators" of discrimination, and appoint a person in each school to monitor implementation of the new programs.*

Clearly, the sodomites currently have an agenda to brainwash the next generation of America. Their target is the young person!

In 1814, Sir John David McCaliss did a comprehensive study on homosexuality in which he concluded: *"Whoever wishes to ruin a nation has only to get the vice of sodomy introduced. For it is extremely difficult to excavate it, where it has once taken root and once it has footing in any country, however powerful and flourishing, we may venture as politicians to predict that the foundation of its future decline is laid, and that after some hundred years it will no longer be the same powerful country it is at present."*

Barbaric Russian leader Joseph Stalin sought to destroy America during the Cold War and to replace it with Communism as the dominate world power. He reflected, *"America is like a healthy body and its resistance is threefold: its patriotism, its morality and its spiritual life. If we can undermine these three areas, America will collapse from within."* America is being destroyed as its morality is undermined in the lives, hearts, and minds of our youth.

For over the past 60 years, there has been a systematic and strategic attack upon our Judeo-Christian values, as well as upon our rich American heritage, by brainwashing the future generations of America with heresy and revised history! Dr. Paul Vitz, a New York University psychology professor, conducted a research for the United States Department of Education on the sixty most accepted textbooks in the public schools that 87% of American youth were using. His stunning discovery revealed that there was *a total absence of Christianity in the books.* Though other religions were referenced, *not one time* was anything mentioned concerning the Bible-believing faith of our founding fathers or other notable Americans throughout our history. Furthermore, children are learning about the "importance" of the Seneca Falls Convention advocating women's rights rather than the significance of Lincoln's Gettysburg Address. They seem to know about someone like Mansa Musa, a 14th century West African king, yet remain clueless to the names Paul Revere or Robert E. Lee. This is only the beginning! Public school history books are replacing our founding fathers and national heroes with various celebrities and public icons, such as Marilyn Monroe among others. Other steps have been taken to purposefully thwart truth and change history, such as teaching that Thomas Jefferson fathered a number of children by one of his slave girls!

Our country will collapse if Christianity is extinguished and morality is snuffed out…if the Truth is not taught. John Adams said, *"We have no government armed with power capable of contending with human passions unbridled with morality and religion. Avarice, ambition, revenge or gallantry would break the strongest cords of our Constitution as a whale goes through a net. Our Constitution was made only for a moral and religious people. It is wholly inadequate to the government of any other."*

We must join the rally cry of Samuel Adams, who said, *"Let statesmen and patriots unite their endeavors to renovate the age by educating their little boys and girls and leading them in the study and practice of the exalted virtues of the Christian system."* We must educate the next generation with Bible-believing Christianity and morality!

William Murray, Madalyn O'Hair's son, lived a pitiful and unfulfilled life until he rejected atheism and Marxism and turned to the Lord Jesus Christ. In 1980, he wrote a letter of apology to the American people:

> *"First, I would like to apologize to the people…for whatever part I played in the removal of Bible reading and praying from the public schools.… I now realize the value of this great tradition and the importance it has played in the past in keeping America a moral and lawful country. I can now see the damage this removal has caused to our nation in the form of loss of faith and moral decline…. Being raised an atheist, I was not aware of faith or even the existence of God. As I now look back at over thirty three years of life wasted without faith in God, I pray only that I can, with His help, right some of the wrong and evil I have caused through my lack of faith…. If it were in my personal power to help return this nation to its rightful place by placing God back in the classroom, I would do so…"*

In May of 1998, William Murray, now the chairman of the "Religious Freedom Coalition," was asked on CBN's *700 Club, "It was, of course, your Supreme Court case that removed prayer from schools almost four decades ago. What do you think have been the consequences of that decision?"*

He replied, *"[The government is] surely not neutral toward religion as our Founding Fathers intended. Their idea of neutrality is actually anti-Christian and anti-religious in nature, which is to be expected. What we really took out of the schools in 1963 with this case was not prayer but the presence of the authority of God. They tried to replace that. Educators tried to replace it with the authority of the logic of mankind, which immediately failed, and what we've had to do is to replace that in our schools with the iron fist of government. So what we actually have replaced the freedom that goes along with Christianity, we have replaced with a totalitarian system in our schools."*

William Murray warned us by continuing to say that, *"...you are going to see the ACLU and all of these other far-left organizations not only continue but escalate in their attacks against religious freedom in America. ... [T]he ACLU, the PAW, Norman Lear and all his Hollywood perverts that fund these attacks on religious liberty in America will be emboldened,..."* if we do not lift up our voices and make a stand for our freedoms!

UNDERSTANDING THE CONSTITUTION
The Education of our Youth in the Science of Government

Housed in the National Archives Building in Washington D.C., lies one of the most unique documents in the world. It is our "roadmap," our "blueprint," by which our government is to be operated. It is the formula for national success, which if any nation followed, would produce a Biblical standard of government and thereby liberty and great prosperity. It is a document based on the Bible and, thus far in our history, **has not granted but has guaranteed** us our way of life and has made our country the most unique nation in the world.

Our liberties are given to us by God. As we have already studied, Thomas Jefferson wrote in our Declaration for Independence that *"all men are created equal and that they are endowed by their Creator with certain unalienable rights, among these are life, liberty, and the pursuit of happiness."*

This was one of the ways the Bible was involved in the forming of our nation, government, and constitution – providing that basic tri-fold premise of our War for Independence…what our founding fathers believed was worth dying for:

Life – Genesis 2:7 says, *"And the LORD God formed man of the dust of the ground, and breathed into his nostrils the breath of life; and man became a living soul."*

Liberty – II Corinthians 3:17 says, *"where the Spirit of the Lord is, there is liberty."* Psalm 119:45 says, *"And I will walk at liberty: for I seek thy precepts."* Our Founding Fathers recognized that if God and His Word were in the center of their thoughts and conduct, they would walk in liberty – because this was something secured to them in promises from Jehovah God. Isaac Backus, a leading preacher in the pulpits during the War for Independence, in a sermon in 1773 reflected that *true liberty* of a man is *"to know, obey and enjoy his Creator, and to do all the good unto, and enjoy the happiness with and in his fellow-creatures that he is capable of."*

Pursuit of Happiness – Ecclesiastics 3:13 says, *"And also that every man should eat and drink, and enjoy the good of all his labour, it is the gift of God."* Ecclesiastics 5:19 also says, *"Every man also to whom God hath given riches and wealth, and hath given him power to eat thereof, and to take his portion, and to rejoice in his labour; this is the gift of God."* Psalm 146:5, *"Happy is he that hath the God of Jacob for his help, whose hope is in the LORD his God:"* Proverbs 16:20 says, *"Whoso trusteth in the LORD, happy is he."* Proverbs 29:18 says, *"He that keepeth the law, happy is he."*

The fact that the War for Independence was founded upon life, liberty, and the pursuit of happiness shows that it was born of God. God birthed within our forefathers' hearts these precepts and principles of Biblical freedom. That is why there is a movement in our country to eradicate God *out of the national consciousness* – taking Him *out of the pledge* of our flag, taking *our trust in Him off of our currency*, taking Him *out of our history*, and *removing His commandments* from our courtrooms. If the government can persuade WE THE PEOPLE that *they* – the government – are the ones who give us our rights and not God, then they can take those liberties away from us. We do not receive these rights from our government. Woodrow Wilson said, *"Liberty has never come from government. The history of liberty is a history of limitations of governmental power, not the increase of it."* Our government was instituted to secure these rights, to guarantee these rights granted to us by God. Thomas Jefferson wrote in the Declaration of Independence that to SECURE these rights, governments are instituted among men – **THAT** is the role of government. Our country was founded upon principles of liberty from the hand of God, not the hand of government. To say that the government gives us our rights and not God is Biblically and historically incorrect.

THE CONSTITUTION & THE DECLARATION OF INDEPENDENCE

Our Founding Fathers developed the Constitution in the light of the Declaration of Independence. The Constitution was written in relation to our "nation's birth certificate" for a two-fold purpose: to ensure those principles of freedom stated in our Declaration and to fix the grievances that we made toward Great Britain and its tyranny so that it would not happen in our country with our government.

The Constitution of the United States and the Declaration of Independence work perfectly hand-in-hand. In 1776, the Declaration of Independence stated America's foundational principles of liberty, justice, and dependency upon God; and, the Constitution reinforces everything stated and fought for by setting the rules and guidelines by which our newborn country would be operated. The Declaration of Independence is the "why" for who we are as a country, and the Constitution is the "how" for the way it is to continue in liberty and prosperity. The United States Supreme Court explained in 1897: *"The first official action of this nation declared the foundation of government in these words: 'We hold these truths to be self-evident, that all men are created equal, that they are endowed by their Creator with certain unalienable rights, that among these are life, liberty, and the pursuit of happiness.' While such declaration of principles may not have the force of organic law, or be made the basis of judicial decision as to the limits of right and duty, and while in all cases reference must be had to the organic law of the nation for such limits, yet the latter is but the body and the letter of which the former is the thought and the spirit, and **it is always safe to read the letter of the Constitution in the spirit of the Declaration of Independence.**"*

The Constitution cannot be understood without the Declaration of Independence. The Constitution was never to be interpreted apart from those values expressed in the Declaration. Well into the 20ᵗʰ century, the Declaration and the Constitution were viewed as inseparable and interdependent with each other. However, in recent times, liberals and judicial activists have changed this and are trying to completely sever the connection. *We must spread the truth of what is happening.* The Constitution provided the specific details of how the American government should operate under the principles set forth in the Declaration.

THE ORGANIZATION OF THE CONSTITUTION

So what exactly is the Constitution? It is the document setting forth the principles on which our government was originally formed and now must continue to be conducted and operated. It is the textbook to our "science of government," our instruction manual for how to do things correctly.

The process of creating a constitution begins with the voluntary association of men in sufficient numbers to form a political community. Enough representatives from each state must be present, to accurately portray the population from each part of the country.

The first step to be taken for their own security and happiness is to agree on the terms on which they are to be united and to act. To simplify, it is as if they make a long list of goals and principles they wish to establish in their government. Each item is discussed and voted upon, and from this list they begin to form a "plan of government", suited to their character, their needs, and their future prospects. This "plan of government" begins to form into a constitutional outline, article by article, section by section. When it is finalized, they vote on whether this "plan" is what they wish to live by, and they agree that it will be the supreme rule of obligation among them – thus, laying the foundation of the nation's safety, permanency, and happiness.

It is important for us to remember that our Founding Fathers looked at models of governments in history's past, but none seemed to suit their needs in creating our great union. They realized they had to begin from scratch. They argued for five and a half weeks and got nowhere – just "spinning their wheels" and becoming frustrated with one another. Ben Franklin stood and asked in his dramatic speech, *"Why have we, as a unit and assembly together, not once thought of humbly applying to the Father of Lights for wisdom and guidance?"* Smitten in their hearts, our founding fathers put their differences aside, went across the street to a church and prayed and fasted for three days and three nights, beseeching God for forgiveness and wisdom. They came back together after that time, and for the next five weeks they prayed every morning and remained yielded to the direction and leadership of Jehovah God, and they successfully wrote our "plan of government" – the Constitution.

We must never forget that "WE THE PEOPLE" have the greatest example of human government invention, sound political principles, and judicious combinations in our Constitution because it was based upon constant dependency on the leadership, guidance, and wisdom of Jehovah God. Our Constitution is deemed as near to perfection as any document ever formulated for a government. It was birthed and written out of a very unique background – a background of sacrifice, service, and sacred prayer.

THE BIBLE IN THE CONSTITUTION

In 1892, roughly 120 years ago and about 120 years after the formulation of our nation and Constitution, the Supreme Court stated: *"Our laws and our institutions must necessarily be based upon and embody the teachings of the Redeemer of mankind. It is impossible that it should be otherwise; and in this sense and to this extent our civilization and our institutions are emphatically Christian."*

James McHenry, a member of the Continental Congress and a signer of the Constitution, said that the Holy Scriptures *"can alone secure to society, order and peace, and to our courts of justice and constitutions of government, purity, stability, and usefulness."* This is why our forefathers established a nation based upon the Word of God and prayer. An early House Judiciary Committee declared: *"Christianity was the religion of the founders of the republic, and they expected it to remain the religion of their descendants."*

Our Constitution was drafted so as to be in accordance with the Scriptures, to be the legal foundation of a republican form of government based on that model which God had ordained for the children of Israel found in Exodus 18:21, *"Moreover thou shalt provide out of all the people able men, such as fear God, men of truth, hating covetousness; and place such over them, to be rulers of thousands, and rulers of hundreds, rulers of fifties, and rulers of tens:"*

This raises a topic a large number of American are confused about. Are we a Constitutional republic or a Constitutional democracy? And why? James Madison explained in his writings *The Federalist Papers #14: "It is that in a democracy the people meet and exercise the government in person; in a republic they assemble and administer it by their representatives and agents. A democracy, consequently, must be confined to a small pot. A republic may be extended over a large region."* A republic is a structured form of government governed by the people through their elected delegates; however, a democracy is "mob rule." Our Founding Fathers realized that *"God is not the author of confusion"* and decided to implement a system that would operate smoothly under the tenants and through the wisdom of the Word of God. General Nathaniel Freeman explained in 1802, *"Our government originating in the voluntary compact of a people who in that very instrument profess the Christian religion, it may be considered, not a republic like Rome was, a Pagan but a Christian republic."*

Our Founding Fathers wanted to establish a government with three branches, based upon the Divine roles of Jehovah God Himself, as found in Isaiah 33:22: *"For the LORD is our judge* (the judicial branch), *the LORD is our lawgiver* (the legislative branch), *the LORD is our king* (the executive branch); *he will save us."* Among these three branches, they realized they needed to have "separation of powers" (all three branches of government being separate from each other; however, none are independent, but all are accountable to the people) because of what the Bible says in Jeremiah 17:9 – *"The heart is deceitful above all things, and desperately wicked: who can know it?"* Our forefathers knew the wickedness of their own hearts and therefore decided to implement a system of "checks and balances" into our Constitution to secure liberty and republicanism in the generations to follow. Quoting from James Madison in *Federalist Papers #51: "If men were angels,"* the three divisions of power written into our Constitution would not have been necessary.

The Founding Fathers used Biblical principles throughout the Constitution. Article One, Section Eight deals with "Uniform Immigration Laws" in accordance with Leviticus 19:34, *"But the stranger that dwelleth with you shall be unto you as one born among you, and thou shalt love him as thyself; for ye were strangers in the land of Egypt: I am the LORD your God."* America's borders have always been open for anyone and everyone to come from abroad and enjoy our liberties and establish a new home based upon capitalism. This wonderful freedom we share in our ancestry is based upon this tenant from the Word of God.

Article Two, Section One declares that the President of the United States must be a natural born citizen, based on Deuteronomy 17:15, *"Thou shalt in any wise set him king over thee, whom the LORD thy God shall choose: one from among thy brethren shalt thou set king over thee: thou mayest not set a stranger over thee, which is not thy brother."* This raises the question: Is President Barack Obama a true citizen of the United States? A lot of people have heard rumors about this but have never heard the weighing evidence and details. Let's discuss it for a few moments. This is very, very important. If Mr. Obama is not a natural born citizen, he must be removed from his oval office by direct order from the Constitution. This principle is founded upon the Bible.

Philip J. Berg – a licensed attorney, a former deputy attorney general of Pennsylvania, and a Democrat for many years – is the "main man" attempting to bring this case before the Supreme Court to ensure that our Constitution is being upheld. Mr. Berg filed a federal lawsuit against President Obama, claiming that he is *not* a natural born citizen and was therefore ineligible for the presidency. The case required Obama to present birth documents proving otherwise, but Obama would not comply. Mr. Berg said, *"As a life-long democrat, I am really dismayed that Obama will not produce records to prove me wrong."* Berg argues that President Obama was born in Kenya in 1961 to an American woman, Stanley Ann Dunham, and a Kenyan man, Barack Hussein Obama Sr., *as reportedly shown by a birth certificate from Mombasa Maternity Hospital* and *witnessed by Obama's own parental grandmother and relatives.* According to the law at that time, a parent could pass United

States citizenship on to a child born abroad if the parent was at least 19 years old. **However,** *Obama's mother was only 18 years old.* No hospital birth certificate has been produced to prove Obama was born in Hawaii, only a certificate of birth registry **after the fact,** which forensics experts have denounced as a forgery. New photos of his birth certificate were posted on the Internet by *FactCheck.org,* which "supposedly" checks out the validity of documents to ensure they are correct. *FactCheck.org* says that this birth certificate IS a true document, but this company is owned by Annenberg of Chicago. Annenberg of Chicago has been a very faithful sponsor and supporter of Obama, since he was one of its board members for a number of years. Is there a "conflict of interest" here? It is quite suspicious in itself that the "facts" were not "checked" by an *independent* source and that only a short-form birth certificate without the name of the Hawaii hospital has been given. When interviewed, President Obama claimed he was born at one hospital in Hawaii while his half-sister, when interviewed, claimed he was born in a different hospital in Hawaii. *Supposedly Obama was born in three different hospitals?* Things do not seem to be adding up. When a person tells the truth, everything is always the same; but when someone lies or tries to cover something up, their facts are all over the place and are not consistent as they should be. **This is what we are seeing here.** Moreover, when Obama was six years old his mother remarried and moved with her husband to his home country of Indonesia. Records indicate Obama was naturalized as an Indonesian citizen and put into a Muslim elementary school. Indonesia does not allow dual nationality, so even if Obama *had* been born in Hawaii, he would have *lost* his citizenship then as a child. He would no longer be a natural-born citizen; he would be a naturalized citizen, and **nationalized citizens can NOT run for the United States Presidency.** Obama has also refused to release his medical or college records from Columbia University and Harvard Law School. *This is significant because these documents might reveal his citizenship.* If President Obama is a truly a natural born citizen – what is he trying to hide?

Article Three, Section Three deals with the witnesses required for capital punishment, directly in line with Deuteronomy 17:6, *"At the mouth of two witnesses, or three witnesses, shall he that is worthy of death be put to death; but at the mouth of one witness he shall not be put to death."*

And there are many other principles in the Constitution's articles that were taken from the Bible, such as provision against an attainder (Ezekiel 18:20), tax exemption for churches (Ezra 7:24), and more.

BREAKDOWN OF THE CONSTITUTION

PREAMBLE
ARTICLE 1 – *The Legislative Branch*
 SECTION 1 – *The Legislature*
 SECTION 2 – *The House*
 SECTION 3 – *The Senate*
 SECTION 4 – *Elections, Meetings*
 SECTION 5 – *Membership, Rules, Journals, Adjournment*
 SECTION 6 – *Compensation*
 SECTION 7 – *Revenue Bills, Legislative Process, Presidential Veto*
 SECTION 8 – *Powers of Congress*
 SECTION 9 – *Limits on Congress*
 SECTION 10 – *Powers Prohibited of States*
ARTICLE 2 – *The Executive Branch*
 SECTION 1 – *The President*
 SECTION 2 – *Civilian Power over Military, Cabinet, Pardon Power, Appointments*
 SECTION 3 – *State of the Union, Convening Congress*
 SECTION 4 – *Disqualification*
ARTICLE 3 – *The Judicial Branch*
 SECTION 1 – *Judicial Powers*
 SECTION 2 – *Trial by Jury, Original Jurisdiction, Jury Trials*
 SECTION 3 – *Treason*
ARTICLE 4 – *The States*
 SECTION 1 – *Each State to Honor All Others*
 SECTION 2 – *State Citizens, Extradition*
 SECTION 3 – *New States*
 SECTION 4 – *Republican Government*

THE WORKINGS OF THE CONSTITUTION

Our government is divided into three branches: the legislative, the executive, and the judicial. Each one has its own role in how laws are made and used; however, they are joined together with "checks and balances." No one branch has more power than the other; however, the weakest of the three should be the judiciary.

The **Legislative Branch** makes the law. The legislature is called the Congress, and it is split into two parts – the House of Representatives and the Senate. In the "House," each representative comes from a district in one of the states. The representative's job is to represent the people in that district who elected him to voice their thoughts, opinions, and concerns. We have the right to tell our representatives how we feel about issues. There are 435 representatives all together. Bigger states have more representatives than the smaller ones, but every state has at least one. The Senate, however, has only 100 senators. There are two senators from each state. "We the people" also elect the senators, and they are to represent our interests, as well. When the Congress wants to pass a law, both the House and the Senate must agree by majority vote to the exact same law. If they cannot agree, the law cannot be passed.

The **Executive Branch** is designed primarily to make sure that the law is carried out correctly. The President heads up this branch of our government. The Executive Branch also consists of the Vice President and the Secretaries of all the departments in the President's cabinet. Before a new law can be formed, the President must agree to it. If he does not agree, he rejects (vetoes) the law. This is an example of how the "checks and balances" work. The Congress must pass laws the President will agree to. However, the President is accountable for his decisions regarding laws.

The **Judiciary Branch** is to interpret the law correctly according to and only by the Constitution of the United States.

THE BILL OF RIGHTS

It is interesting how we originally received our first Ten Amendments to the Constitution, which we call *"The Bill of Rights."*

As we studied, God's men intensely fought for freedom and debated the points of liberty in Independence Hall and Continental Congress. Their preaching was responsible for setting aflame the hearts of the America people for independence and freedom. One such preacher that made an incredible difference for all Americans was a man by the name of John Leland.

John Leland was one of the most influential Baptist preachers and champions of religious liberty. As our new nation was formed, he was highly concerned with the preservation of our freedoms. He was able to meet with James Madison, to discuss Madison's candidacy for Virginia delegate to the convention to ratify our Constitution. At that meeting, Leland expressed the importance of religious freedom and individual rights based upon the Bible. Madison promised Leland that if he was elected, he would do all in his power to see these freedoms incorporated into the Constitution by amendment. True to his word, Madison drafted and introduced twelve amendments to our Constitution – the Bill of Rights. Interestingly, two men who greatly helped Madison in the formulation of these freedoms were George Mason of the Constitutional Convention and Frederick Muhlenberg, the brother of Pastor/General Peter Muhlenberg from Woodstock, Virginia.

THE PENMAN OF THE CONSTITUTION

Gouverneur Morris is one man who revisionist historians have tried their best to "sweep under the rug" and forget about. His name was removed from mainstream public history books over eighty years ago, even though he was one of the most important men involved with the writing of the Constitution – *he was the very penman of it himself*. He spoke more than other delegate during the Constitutional Convention – 173 times – mostly concerning how God and the Bible played a foundational role in the establishment of our colonies and our new-born nation. He also made other bold statements such as: *"Americans need never fear their government because of the advantage of being armed, which the Americans possess over the people of almost every other nation."* And, *"This magistrate is not the king. The people are the king."* Gouverneur

Morris understood that "WE THE PEOPLE" are the government through its republic form and the elected representative are our servants working for us.

CHAPTER VII

THE NECESSITY OF A REMNANT
Saving America Before it is Too Late

This is a critical hour in which we find ourselves living. However, *God makes the brightest lights to shine in the darkest of nights.* In order to shine effectively and unhindered, however, we must know the truth. The truth for every human being is, first and foremost, the Bible. Secondly, the truth for every American is the Constitution that was based upon dependency on Jehovah God. We must know what those truths are so that we can shine as beacons in a very dark time in our nation's history. God did not allow Billy Sunday, D.L. Moody, George Washington, or Patrick Henry to live today – He has given us the opportunity and the responsibility. Therefore, He will most definitely grant us the power and give us the guidance and discernment we need to be an effective witness. There is a dire need for us to maintain the cause, so that we can continue to see the Gospel of our Lord Jesus Christ go forward and our liberties be preserved.

George Washington said, *"Of all the dispositions and habits which lead to political prosperity, religion and morality are indispensable supports."* The Word of God and living pure, clean, holy lives that glorify God are two direct foundation pillars that will allow our United States of America to continue on with healthy prosperity and success. That means if those two pillars are removed, we will begin to crumble. Psalm 11:3 says, *"If the foundations be destroyed, what can the righteous do?"*

However, in today's society, we widely see a lack of knowledge about true "religion" or Bible-believing Christianity. What we mean by "Bible-believing" Christianity is the belief that the Bible is the inspired, preserved Word of God for us, and we will follow everything that God tells us to do in His Word. We will not add our own thoughts to His Word or take away from It things we think are unnecessary. Most denominations of Christianity and religion in general are watered down with a little element of truth mixed with a majority of man-made philosophies and theological principles. Some religions – such as Islam, Buddhism, Hinduism, Shintoism, Atheism, Agnosticism, Deism, Roman Catholicism, Mormonism, Christian Scientism, and Jehovah's Witness dogma – are not even true at all. We as a nation are far removed from true Bible-believing "religion." One of our main pillars for national success and prosperity has been broken down. Statistics prove this – 35% of my parents' generation go to a church faithfully whatever type of denomination or religion that may be. A smaller percent of that are involved with true Bible-believing churches. The problem is with my generation – only 4% of my generation is currently going to any church of any denomination or religion. We are at a serious crossroads. Our national hope is crumbling quickly.

In today's society, we also see a widespread lack of morality. Many dress immodestly or "sexy" in such a way that it draws inappropriate attention to parts of the body. Hollywood, movies, television shows, video games, music videos, and music is loaded with immorality, ill-clad men and women, innuendos of sexual relationships, pornography, and other wicked impure things. This is not morality. Morality is remaining pure, chaste, and undefiled. Morality is dressing appropriately to not excite lust in the opposite sex. Morality is living a good, sensible, respectable, and clean life. We are greatly lacking this in today's youth and culture. This "pillar" of national success and hope is falling away, and we as a nation will soon feel the consequences of this collapse. We cannot ignore God and the Bible!

God says in Hosea 5:6 (speaking of Israel, though it can readily and easily be applied to America – We could be "considered" as "God's people" since America was the only other nation besides

Israel in the history of the world to base itself upon Jehovah God and His Word), *"My people are destroyed for lack of knowledge: because thou hast rejected knowledge, I will also reject thee,...: seeing thou hast forgotten the law of thy God, I will also forget thy children."* If we want any hope in this country for the next generation, we must no longer forget the Word of God but must be submersed in it once again, learn it, and preach it. We are being destroyed because of a lack of knowledge and the rejection of knowledge when it is brought to our attention. But God is merciful. He always gives a space of grace. We are in its final hour, but we must hear His pleading cry to us as a nation in Jeremiah 2:9, *"Wherefore I will yet plead with you, saith the LORD, and with your children's children will I plead."*

God does not want us destroyed, so He will tell the truth to us plain and simple. In verse 11b, He states: *"but my people have changed their glory for that which doth not profit."* We have changed ourselves from Bible-believing Christianity and morality to humanistic thinking and provocative looseness – thinking that we can still succeed as a nation. We will only truly find the concept of profit in the Word of God. Our founding fathers knew this. That is why they decided to created a union and a constitution based upon the principles and precepts of God's Word. They knew the truth of Joshua 1:8, *"This book of the law shall not depart out of thy mouth; but thou shalt meditate therein day and night, that thou mayest observe to do according to all that is written therein: for then thou shalt make thy way prosperous, and then thou shalt have good success."*

God continues to say in Jeremiah 2:13, *"For my people have committed two evils; they have forsaken me the fountain of living waters, and hewed them out cisterns, broken cisterns, that can hold no water."* Today, we have forsaken the Bible and God, thinking that we can do it all ourselves without His help or guidance and that He is just a myth and His Book is just a bunch of fairy tales or stories with good morals that we can learn from. We have made ourselves "wells" – forms of reasoning, government, and entertainment – that cannot hold "water," the Water of Life which is God and His Word. These are two grave mistakes.

Because we have done this, Jeremiah 2:15 is coming to pass: *"The young lions roared upon him, and yelled, and they made his land waste: his cities are burned without inhabitant."* The demons of Hell have come through various means of infiltration in media, humanstic philosophies, and other ways and are destroying the very fabric of our existance, our family units, our government, and our young people. Why would they try to destroy our young people by withholding them from true Bible-believing Christianity and tempting them to immorality as we discussed a few paragraphs ago? The reasoning is two-fold. One, so that there will remain no one to be true future guardians of liberty; two, so that they will inherit a nation crumbling away without its two essential pillars of national prosperity. We are in the transformation stage in our country – in the current process of foundations being torn, stripped away, and broken down. Once the foundations are gone, there is nothing more that we will be able to do. So let's *do* something now while we still have the chance. If we don't, we will soon be as God describes – *"waste...and burned without inhabitant."*

Remember what Daniel Webster said? *"If we abide by the principles taught in the Bible, our country will go on prospering and to prosper; If we and our posterity shall be true to the Christian religion, if we and they shall live always in the fear of God and shall respect His commandments, we may have the highest hopes of the future fortunes of our country. But if we and our posterity neglect religious instruction and authority; violate the rules of eternal justice, trifle with the injunctions of morality, and recklessly destroy the political constitution which holds us together, no man can tell how sudden a catastrophe may overwhelm us and bury all our glory in profound obscurity."* He knew of this danger and tried his best to warn us of the consequences. Ladies and gentlemen, young people – we have already neglected God and "religious" instruction, violated the rules, trifled with immorality, and are currently recklessly destroying our Constitution. I fear that we are about to witness a very catastrophic disaster that will bury us into dark, cold, smothering obscurity!

In Deuteronomy 8:11 & 19, God warns us, *"Beware that thou forget not the LORD thy God, in not keeping his commandments, and his judgments, and his statutes, which I command thee this day... And it shall be, if thou do at all forget the LORD thy God, and walk after other gods, and serve them, and worship them, I testify against you this day that ye shall surely perish."*

God asks us, reasoning with us in Jeremiah 2:17, *"Hast thou not procured this unto thyself, in that thou hast forsaken the LORD thy God, when he led thee by the way?"* He makes a concluding statement in the last part of verse 19, *"know therefore and see that it is an evil thing and bitter, that thou hast forsaken the LORD thy God."*

When we have complete forsaken and forgotten Him, we will be turned into hell. Psalm 9:17 says, *"The wicked shall be turned into hell, and all the nations that forget God."*

I believe America is on this road of catastrophe. It is very imminent…we are on the brink of destruction and of collapse! We are living in a time:

- ✓ When drugs are widespread – young people smoking their first cigarettes at young teen ages, etc.
- ✓ Alcohol is flowing freely in the streets – children are able to access open bottles from off the coffee table
- ✓ Immorality and teen abortions are on the continual rise
- ✓ Gangs are becoming more popular and dominant among youth
- ✓ Churches are losing their barriers of separation and becoming more like the world
- ✓ Evolution and socialism are taught as doctrine in the public schools – brainwashing the next generation with principles that are opposite those of our Founding Fathers
- ✓ Rebellion among teens is becoming more prevalent
- ✓ More and more young people are dressing like Goths and punk rockers
- ✓ Music videos on television are very obscene with nudity and illicit dancing – and are easily viewed by young children, who will imitate the moves and motions they see from them
- ✓ Young people are running away and doing their own thing
- ✓ Television itself is become more vulgar and graphic
- ✓ Young people lose their virginity at the average age of **13 years old**
- ✓ Video games are loaded with bloody violence and gore, nudity, sexual themes, drug content, language, witchcraft, and things that children, young people, or *any* person should not be exposed to

✓ The internet is full of loopholes to access pornography and wickedness – becoming a wide-open portal for young people to easily become defiled at young ages

This generation and America are crumbling apart!

✓ Over **76%** of high school seniors, **70%** of tenth graders, and **54%** of eighth graders are regularly drinking alcohol.

✓ Around **39%** of teenagers have had five or more drinks in a row within one month's period of time.

✓ Nearly **33%** of all seniors are using illicit drugs, about **21%** of them are using marijuana, **7%** take stimulants, **6.2%** are using inhalants, and **5.6%** are using LSD.

✓ Over **30%** of grade school children have already taken their first drink.

✓ On any given weekend, **30%** of teenagers in America are drunk.

✓ AIDS among teenagers has increased **62%** since 1990, and the number of teens with AIDS doubles every 14 months.

✓ Two out of every three teenage boys have had sex by the time they are 18, and on average they have had immoral relationships with at least five different girls.

✓ One out of every three girls between the ages of 15-17 has had sexual intercourse.

✓ The television is on an average of **7 hours and 12 minutes** each day in the American home.

✓ Parents in America only spend an average of **38.5** minutes in meaningful conversation a week with their children.

✓ According to the studies of the Nehemiah Institute, **83%** of all children who grow up in a Christian home but attend a public school will eventually accept a secular rather than spiritual world-view.

✓ The Barna Research Institute informs us that **70%** of children who grow up in a Christian home but attend a public school will depart from the faith of their parents.

Notice what happens *every day* in the life of an American young person:

- ✓ **3,000** children witness the divorce of their parents
- ✓ **3,300** teens run away from home
- ✓ **150** attempt suicide (third leading cause of death for young people)
- ✓ **450** teens arrested for drinking
- ✓ **210** teens arrested for drug related crimes
- ✓ **2,860** teens drop out of school
- ✓ **1,630** teens are admitted to adult jails
- ✓ **7,750** teens become sexually active
- ✓ **1,110** teen girls become pregnant
- ✓ **8,220** teens acquire a STD (sexually transmitted disease)

These statistics just given are not from last year, not from five years ago…but are from 1995! I'm afraid this is just the scratch on the surface – it is very likely that much more than what has been reported here is going on across America today!

Does your heart not BURN within you?

God asks in Ezekiel 8:17, *"Hast thou seen this, O son of man? IS IT A LIGHT THING to the house of Judah that they commit the abominations which they commit here?"* Is it a light thing to our country that we commit such wickedness before the eyes of God? To realize that we were based upon the Bible, prayer, and the guidance and wisdom of God, and yet have cast it all away these past 60 years and go in our own direction.

IS IT A LIGHT THING in America that we are KILLING innocent children? Do you realize that we have murdered over 49 million babies since we "legalized" abortion in this country? Satan is trying to MURDER and DESTROY our FUTURE!

IS IT A LIGHT THING that they are CORRUPTING the minds of our young people? Satan is trying to MARR and VIOLATE the preciousness and purity of the next generation!

IS IT A LIGHT THING that churches are COMPROMISING and becoming MORE like the world? Satan is trying to make our young people CRAVE the pleasures of sin that will only last for a season and then leave them RUINED!

IS IT A LIGHT THING that they are CALLING upon false "gods" (of money, government, etc.) for HELP – just as the children of Israel did? Satan is trying to MAGNIFY the things of the world over the things of God!

BUT I BELIEVE THAT AMERICA IS STILL WORTH SAVING! But do we understand what threats we are facing? We must understand the times just as the Bible says in Romans 13:11, *"...knowing the time...that NOW it is HIGH TIME to AWAKE out of SLEEP:"*

If there has ever been a time in the history of America when God needs young people and Christians to stand and make a difference – it is today. Because we are living in special times, God needs special Christians, special young people who are going to have the same resolve down deep in their soul as our Founding Fathers. Young people who are going to "grit their teeth" and say that there is something worth fighting for!

Our Founding Fathers said, *"For the support of this declaration, with a firm reliance on the protection of the Divine Providence, we mutually pledge to each other, our lives, our fortunes, and our sacred honor."* We need to mentally have this kind of determination. Liberals are advancing. Muslims are advancing. Sodomites are advancing. Revisionist historians are advancing. Judicial activists are advancing. *They advance to completely take away our God-given freedoms and liberties.* It is time that young people across this nation realized that they have been ordained of God to become future guardians of liberty and must stand up and fight for what is right!

I would like to ask you a question – a question drawn from Scripture in II Peter 3:11, which God asks Christians as we approach the end of these dark days: *"What manner of persons ought ye to be in all holy conversation and godliness?"* Seeing the issues at hand, seeing the problems in our country with our government and our next generation, what type of Americans – of Christians – ought we to be?

We must be **people of CHARACTER**. We must have the character of Naboth as found in I Kings 21. Naboth lived next door to Israel's vile King Ahab. Ahab loved Naboth's property, and the more time passed, the more jealous, greedy, and covetous Ahab became.

One day while Naboth was out tending his beautiful vineyard, Ahab strolled over to the fence and called out to him, *"Give me thy vineyard, that I may have it for a garden of herbs, because it is near unto my house: and I will give thee for it a better vineyard than it; or, if it seem good to thee, I will give thee the worth of it in money."* Naboth thought for a moment, still on his knees working on some flowers. He slowly stood, brushed the dark soil on his fingers back into the pretty flower bed, looked up at Ahab who was gazing after him with evil eyes, and said: *"The LORD forbid it me, that I should give the inheritance of my fathers unto thee."* Naboth refused to give away his heritage. He was a man of determined character.

The Bible says in Proverbs 23:23, *"Buy the truth, and sell it not; also wisdom, and instruction, and understanding."* Don't sell out! Our government, now corrupted with liberal agendas and socialistic philosophies, is trying slowly but surely to take away our liberties and our true history. Stand! Be a young man or woman of character and refuse, as Naboth, to give away your heritage! They will try to bribe us. They will try to lie to us that they will exchange it for something better and greater. You cannot replace our Christian heritage and liberties that our Founding Fathers have given to us.

Naboth died for what he rightfully believed. Are you willing to make the ultimate sacrifice as a person of character? Protect your freedom and your faith to the very end – even unto death!

Don't have the character of Esau, who sold His blessing of God for temporary satisfaction. Hebrews 12:16-17 says, *"Lest there be any fornicator, or profane person, as Esau, who for one morsel of meat sold his birthright. For ye know how that afterward, when he would have inherited the blessing, he was rejected: for he found no place of repentance, though he sought it carefully with tears."* Once he gave it away, he could not get it back, even though the Bible says *"he sought it carefully with tears."* Once we give away our freedoms to the enemy, we will not be able to retrieve them.

We must say as our Founding Fathers: *"We hold these truths to be self evident."* We must be people of character like Naboth, who refused to give away his heritage and his family vineyard to the enemy. We must hold the principles of life, liberty, and the pursuit of happiness. The liberal world is trying to remove them from us – pry our fingers off them – to <u>FULLY</u> <u>STRIP</u> <u>us</u>. Don't let them go.

We must be **people of COMMITMENT** – committed to God to carry through to the very end, no matter the public opinion. Proverbs 20:6 asks, *"Every man will proclaim his own goodness, but a faithful man who can find?"*

Commit yourself to RECLAIM your country back to the Biblical principles it was founded upon. Get in the fight for your country. Grab hold of the liberties that we share and reject the lies that are being presented to us. It is time for us to "put our foot down" and plant ourselves upon the Bible and the Constitution and say, *"We are not moving. We are reclaiming this ground back again for God and for our Founding Fathers."*

Commit yourself to RENAME sin, wickedness, and wrongdoing taking place openly in our country and in our government. Say what it truly is instead of "whitewashing" it with political correctness. We need to call it what it used to be called!

Commit yourself to REMAIN faithful to God and Country. God asks us to *"Occupy* (stand your ground – don't leave your post) *till I come."* (Luke 19:13) Be faithful in being alert for the enemy and for evil that will destroy our country, and share this truth with others to make them aware of what is going on. Be faithful in being a light for the Lord Jesus Christ in the midst of this dark world, in a day when most Americans do not know for sure if they will be in Heaven when they die. Therefore, we must be the most enthusiastic Christians we can be for our nation. Jesus says in Matthew 5:16, *"Let your light so shine before men, that they may see your good works, and glorify your Father which is in heaven."* We must commit ourselves to remain fruitful and bring *"all men...unto the knowledge of the truth."* (I Timothy 2:4) I Timothy 2:3 says that *"this is good and acceptable in the sight of God our Saviour;"*

We must be **people who will CONTINUE**. God pleads with us in II Timothy 3:14-15, *"But continue thou in the things which thou hast learned and hast been assured of, knowing of whom thou hast learned them; And that from a child thou hast known the holy scriptures, which are able to make thee wise unto salvation through faith which is in Christ Jesus."*

God wants us to continue strong as A SOLDIER. II Timothy 2:3-4 says, *"Thou therefore endure hardness, as a good soldier of Jesus Christ.*

No man that warreth entangleth himself with the affairs of this life; that he may please him who hath chosen him to be a soldier." Stay in the fight! As soldiers of the Cross may we determine and resolve down deep within our own hearts: *"I do solemnly swear that I will support and defend the Constitution of the United States against ALL enemies, foreign and domestic; that I will bear true faith and allegiance to the same; to unashamedly obey the orders of my God and Lord Jesus Christ and follow my authorities as they serve our nation under God. So help me God."* When you grow weak, draw your strength from the Saviour. Isaiah 40:28-31 reasons with us, *"Hast thou not known? hast thou not heard, that the everlasting God, the LORD, the Creator of the ends of the earth, fainteth not, neither is weary? He giveth power to the faint; and to them that have no might he increaseth strength. Even the youths shall faint and be weary, and the young men shall utterly fall: But they that wait upon the LORD shall renew their strength; …they shall run, and not be weary; and they shall walk, and not faint."*

God wants us to continue strong as A SOULWINNER. Christ declares in John 9:4, *"I must work the works of Him that sent me while it is day, the night cometh when no man can work."* Jesus was determined to continue as a witness to the very end – so should we. We must fulfill that Macedonian cry mentioned in Acts 16:9, *"Come over & help us!"* We must answer the pleadful cry of young people desiring to be delivered from the bondage and shackles of this wicked world! We must reach out to "the rich man's five brethren" as mentioned in Luke 16. The rich man looked up and saw the beggar Lazarus standing with Abraham up in Paradise and cried out for mercy and for one drop of water to cool his tongue and ease the pain from the excruciating torments he was suffering. When he realized that nothing could be done for him and that he was eternal damned to suffer this fate for all of eternity – he lifted his voice with a fierce and ferocious cry in the midst of his pain, *"Send Lazarus back from the dead…send somebody back to my father's house to witness to my five brethren so that they don't wind up coming down to this place of torment!"* We must strongly continue as soulwinners for our Lord Jesus Christ. He is the only hope for this country. We must witness while we still have the freedom and we still have the chance. **In order to save America, we must get America saved.**

God wants us to continue strong as A SERVANT. We must be a servant to our fellow man. This is the second commandment Christ gave us: *"Love thy neighbor as thyself."* One of the ways we can be effective servants for our country is by being a good steward of the God-given institution of government, as we mentioned previously. To be a good steward and maintain our country and government, we must understand our Constitution. Once we are informed, we can effectively be **involved**, can effectively **drive away those who wish to harm us and take advantage of us**, and can effectively **instruct others** in the truth of how our government through the Constitution is to be operated. Again, I Corinthians 4:2 says, *"Moreover it is required in stewards that a man be found faithful."* If we do our part and continue strong until the end, we will hear Jehovah God say to us, *"Well done, thou good and faithful servant"* (Matthew 25:21).

What type of an American and Christian are you going to be in these last days…and in these perilous times? Are you going to be found fully faithful to God, your Bible, your country, and your Constitution unto the end? God challenges us in Revelation 2:25, *"But that which ye have already hold fast till I come."* Jesus says in Revelation 3:11, *"Behold, I come quickly: hold that fast which thou hast, that no man take thy crown."* We have something priceless that we cannot give away….

CONCLUSION

I want to give you a challenge. TODAY, get on your knees in a private place and passionately, sincerely beg God to develop you into the Christian and American that you ought to be. Become a full-time Christian for the Lord Jesus Christ and resolve down in the depths of your heart that you will become a part of the remnant who will make an eternal difference in this nation. Determine to restore our country back to the foundational principles of our forefathers concerning religion, morality, and government. Ask God to develop you into someone who will remain committed and continue forward – no matter the cost or the popular opinion – as a soldier, a soulwinner, and a servant. Ask God to mold you into the individual of character and confidence – refusing to lay down the "sword" of truth but earnestly contending until the very end.

Finish this book by carefully reading and studying our Constitution in its entirety for yourself. Also become familiar with the Declaration of Independence – the birth certificate of America. Early patriots and American people have died on battlefields all over this world in order to preserve these documents. Engrain their principles down deep in the innermost being of your mind and your heart, so that you can be a true American. We as Christians memorize God's Word because it is truth. We as *Americans* must also put to memory those government precepts that were based upon the Bible, which we find in our most precious document – our Constitution.

Appendix A: The Declaration of Independence

When, in the course of human events, it becomes necessary for one people to dissolve the political bands which have connected them with another, and to assume among the powers of the earth, the separate and equal station to which the laws of nature and of nature's God entitle them, a decent respect to the opinions of mankind requires that they should declare the causes which impel them to the separation.

We hold these truths to be self-evident, that all men are created equal, that they are endowed by their Creator with certain unalienable rights, that among these are life, liberty and the pursuit of happiness. That to secure these rights, governments are instituted among men, deriving their just powers from the consent of the governed. That whenever any form of government becomes destructive to these ends, it is the right of the people to alter or to abolish it, and to institute new government, laying its foundation on such principles and organizing its powers in such form, as to them shall seem most likely to effect their safety and happiness. Prudence, indeed, will dictate that governments long established should not be changed for light and transient causes; and accordingly all experience hath shown that mankind are more disposed to suffer, while evils are sufferable, than to right themselves by abolishing the forms to which they are accustomed. But when a long train of abuses and usurpations, pursuing invariably the same object evinces a design to reduce them under absolute despotism, it is their right, it is their duty, to throw off such government, and to provide new guards for their future security. --Such has been the patient sufferance of these colonies; and such is now the necessity which constrains them to alter their former systems of government. The history of the present King of Great Britain is a history of repeated injuries and usurpations, all having in direct object the establishment of an absolute tyranny over these states. To prove this, let facts be submitted to a candid world.

✓ He has refused his assent to laws, the most wholesome and necessary for the public good.

✓ He has forbidden his governors to pass laws of immediate and pressing importance, unless suspended in their operation till his assent should be obtained; and when so suspended, he has utterly neglected to attend to them.

✓ He has refused to pass other laws for the accommodation of large districts of people, unless those people would relinquish the right of representation in the legislature, a right inestimable to them and formidable to tyrants only.

✓ He has called together legislative bodies at places unusual, uncomfortable, and distant from the depository of their public records, for the sole purpose of fatiguing them into compliance with his measures.

✓ He has dissolved representative houses repeatedly, for opposing with manly firmness his invasions on the rights of the people.

✓ He has refused for a long time, after such dissolutions, to cause others to be elected; whereby the legislative powers, incapable of annihilation, have returned to the people at large for their exercise; the state remaining in the meantime exposed to all the dangers of invasion from without, and convulsions within.

✓ He has endeavored to prevent the population of these states; for that purpose obstructing the laws for naturalization of foreigners; refusing to pass others to encourage their migration hither, and raising the conditions of new appropriations of lands.

✓ He has obstructed the administration of justice, by refusing his assent to laws for establishing judiciary powers.

✓ He has made judges dependent on his will alone, for the tenure of their offices, and the amount and payment of their salaries.

✓ He has erected a multitude of new offices, and sent hither swarms of officers to harass our people, and eat out their substance.

✓ He has kept among us, in times of peace, standing armies without the consent of our legislature.

✓ He has affected to render the military independent of and superior to civil power.

✓ He has combined with others to subject us to a jurisdiction foreign to our constitution, and unacknowledged by our laws; giving his assent to their acts of pretended legislation:

- For quartering large bodies of armed troops among us:

- For protecting them, by mock trial, from punishment for any murders which they should commit on the inhabitants of these states:

- For cutting off our trade with all parts of the world:

- For imposing taxes on us without our consent:

- For depriving us in many cases, of the benefits of trial by jury:

- For transporting us beyond seas to be tried for pretended offenses:

- For abolishing the free system of English laws in a neighboring province, establishing therein an arbitrary government, and enlarging its boundaries so as to render it at once an example and fit instrument for introducing the same absolute rule in these colonies:

- For taking away our charters, abolishing our most valuable laws, and altering fundamentally the forms of our governments:

- For suspending our own legislatures, and declaring themselves invested with power to legislate for us in all cases whatsoever.

✓   He has abdicated government here, by declaring us out of his protection and waging war against us.

✓   He has plundered our seas, ravaged our coasts, burned our towns, and destroyed the lives of our people.

✓   He is at this time transporting large armies of foreign mercenaries to complete the works of death, desolation and tyranny, already begun with circumstances of cruelty and perfidy scarcely paralleled in the most barbarous ages, and totally unworthy the head of a civilized nation.

✓   He has constrained our fellow citizens taken captive on the high seas to bear arms against their country, to become the executioners of their friends and brethren, or to fall themselves by their hands.

✓   He has excited domestic insurrections amongst us, and has endeavored to bring on the inhabitants of our frontiers, the merciless Indian savages, whose known rule of warfare, is undistinguished destruction of all ages, sexes and conditions.

In every stage of these oppressions we have petitioned for redress in the most humble terms: our repeated petitions have been answered only by repeated injury. A prince, whose character is thus marked by every act which may define a tyrant, is unfit to be the ruler of a free people.

Nor have we been wanting in attention to our British brethren. We have warned them from time to time of attempts by their legislature to extend an unwarrantable jurisdiction over us. We have reminded them of the circumstances of our emigration and settlement here. We have appealed to their native justice and magnanimity, and we have conjured them by the ties of our common kindred to disavow these usurpations, which, would inevitably interrupt our connections and correspondence. They too have been deaf to the voice of justice and of consanguinity. We must, therefore, acquiesce in the necessity, which denounces our separation, and hold them, as we hold the rest of mankind, enemies in war, in peace friends.

We, therefore, the representatives of the United States of America, in General Congress, assembled, appealing to the Supreme Judge of the world for the rectitude of our intentions, do, in the name, and by the authority of the good people of these colonies, solemnly publish and declare, that these united colonies are, and of right ought to be free and independent states; that they are absolved from all allegiance to the British Crown, and that all political connection between them and the state of Great Britain, is and ought to be totally dissolved; and that as free and independent states, they have full power to levy war, conclude peace, contract alliances, establish commerce, and to do all other acts and things which independent states may of right do. And for the support of this declaration, with a firm reliance on the protection of Divine Providence, we mutually pledge to each other our lives, our fortunes and our sacred honor.

DELAWARE
George Read • Caesar Rodney • Thomas McKean

PENNSYLVANIA
George Clymer • Benjamin Franklin • Robert Morris • John Morton • Benjamin Rush • George Ross • James Smith • James Wilson • George Taylor

MASSACHUSETTS
John Adams • Samuel Adams • John Hancock • Robert Treat Paine • Elbridge Gerry

NEW HAMPSHIRE
Josiah Bartlett • William Whipple • Matthew Thornton

RHODE ISLAND
Stephen Hopkins • William Ellery

NEW YORK
Lewis Morris • Philip Livingston • Francis Lewis • William Floyd

GEORGIA
Button Gwinnett • Lyman Hall • George Walton

VIRGINIA
Richard Henry Lee • Francis Lightfoot Lee • Carter Braxton
• Benjamin Harrison • Thomas Jefferson • George Wythe
• Thomas Nelson, Jr.

NORTH CAROLINA
William Hooper • John Penn • Joseph Hewes

SOUTH CAROLINA
Edward Rutledge • Arthur Middleton • Thomas Lynch, Jr.
• Thomas Heyward, Jr.

NEW JERSEY
Abraham Clark • John Hart • Francis Hopkinson • Richard Stockton
• John Witherspoon

CONNECTICUT
Samuel Huntington • Roger Sherman • William Williams • Oliver Wolcott

MARYLAND
Charles Carroll • Samuel Chase • Thomas Stone • William Paca

Appendix B:
The Constitution of the United States of America

Preamble

We the People of the United States, in Order to form a more perfect Union, establish Justice, insure domestic Tranquility, provide for the common defense, promote the general Welfare, and secure the Blessings of Liberty to ourselves and our Posterity, do ordain and establish this Constitution for the United States of America.

Article I

Section 1

All legislative Powers herein granted shall be vested in a Congress of the United States, which shall consist of a Senate and House of Representatives.

Section 2

The House of Representatives shall be composed of Members chosen every second Year by the People of the several States, and the Electors in each State shall have the Qualifications requisite for Electors of the most numerous Branch of the State Legislature.

No Person shall be a Representative who shall not have attained to the Age of twenty five Years, and been seven Years a Citizen of the United States, and who shall not, when elected, be an Inhabitant of that State in which he shall be chosen.

Representatives and direct Taxes shall be apportioned among the several States which may be included within this Union, according to their respective Numbers, which shall be determined by adding to the whole Number of free Persons, including those bound to Service for a Term of Years, and excluding Indians not taxed, three fifths of all other Persons.

The actual Enumeration shall be made within three Years after the first Meeting of the Congress of the United States, and within every subsequent Term of ten Years, in such Manner as they shall by Law direct. The Number of Representatives shall not exceed one for every thirty Thousand, but each State shall have at Least one Representative; and until such enumeration shall be made, the State of New Hampshire shall be entitled to choose three, Massachusetts eight, Rhode Island and Providence Plantations one, Connecticut five, New York six, New Jersey four, Pennsylvania eight, Delaware one, Maryland six, Virginia ten, North Carolina five, South Carolina five and Georgia three.

When vacancies happen in the Representation from any State, the Executive Authority thereof shall issue Writs of Election to fill such Vacancies.

The House of Representatives shall choose their Speaker and other Officers; and shall have the sole Power of Impeachment.

Section 3

The Senate of the United States shall be composed of two Senators from each State, chosen by the Legislature thereof, for six Years; and each Senator shall have one Vote.

Immediately after they shall be assembled in Consequence of the first Election, they shall be divided as equally as may be into three Classes. The Seats of the Senators of the first Class shall be vacated at the Expiration of the second Year, of the second Class at the Expiration of the fourth Year, and of the third Class at the Expiration of the sixth Year, so that one third may be chosen every second Year; and if Vacancies happen by Resignation, or otherwise, during the Recess of the Legislature of any State, the Executive thereof may make temporary Appointments until the next Meeting of the Legislature, which shall then fill such Vacancies.

No person shall be a Senator who shall not have attained to the Age of thirty Years, and been nine Years a Citizen of the United States, and who shall not, when elected, be an Inhabitant of that State for which he shall be chosen.

The Vice President of the United States shall be President of the Senate, but shall have no Vote, unless they be equally divided.

The Senate shall choose their other Officers, and also a President pro tempore, in the absence of the Vice President, or when he shall exercise the Office of President of the United States.

The Senate shall have the sole Power to try all Impeachments. When sitting for that Purpose, they shall be on Oath or Affirmation. When the President of the United States is tried, the Chief Justice shall preside: And no Person shall be convicted without the Concurrence of two thirds of the Members present.

Judgment in Cases of Impeachment shall not extend further than to removal from Office, and disqualification to hold and enjoy any Office of honor, Trust or Profit under the United States: but the Party convicted shall nevertheless be liable and subject to Indictment, Trial, Judgment and Punishment, according to Law.

Section 4

The Times, Places and Manner of holding Elections for Senators and Representatives, shall be prescribed in each State by the

Legislature thereof; but the Congress may at any time by Law make or alter such Regulations, except as to the Place of Choosing Senators.

The Congress shall assemble at least once in every Year, and such Meeting shall be on the first Monday in December, unless they shall by Law appoint a different Day.

Section 5

Each House shall be the Judge of the Elections, Returns and Qualifications of its own Members, and a Majority of each shall constitute a Quorum to do Business; but a smaller number may adjourn from day to day, and may be authorized to compel the Attendance of absent Members, in such Manner, and under such Penalties as each House may provide.

Each House may determine the Rules of its Proceedings, punish its Members for disorderly Behavior, and, with the Concurrence of two-thirds, expel a Member.

Each House shall keep a Journal of its Proceedings, and from time to time publish the same, excepting such Parts as may in their Judgment require Secrecy; and the Yeas and Nays of the Members of either House on any question shall, at the Desire of one fifth of those Present, be entered on the Journal.

Neither House, during the Session of Congress, shall, without the Consent of the other, adjourn for more than three days, nor to any other Place than that in which the two Houses shall be sitting.

Section 6

The Senators and Representatives shall receive a Compensation for their Services, to be ascertained by Law, and paid out of the Treasury of the United States. They shall in all Cases, except Treason, Felony and Breach of the Peace, be privileged from

Arrest during their Attendance at the Session of their respective Houses, and in going to and returning from the same; and for any Speech or Debate in either House, they shall not be questioned in any other Place.

No Senator or Representative shall, during the Time for which he was elected, be appointed to any civil Office under the Authority of the United States which shall have been created, or the Emoluments whereof shall have been increased during such time; and no Person holding any Office under the United States, shall be a Member of either House during his Continuance in Office.

Section 7

All bills for raising Revenue shall originate in the House of Representatives; but the Senate may propose or concur with Amendments as on other Bills.

Every Bill which shall have passed the House of Representatives and the Senate, shall, before it become a Law, be presented to the President of the United States; If he approve he shall sign it, but if not he shall return it, with his Objections to that House in which it shall have originated, who shall enter the Objections at large on their Journal, and proceed to reconsider it. If after such Reconsideration two thirds of that House shall agree to pass the Bill, it shall be sent, together with the Objections, to the other House, by which it shall likewise be reconsidered, and if approved by two thirds of that House, it shall become a Law. But in all such Cases the Votes of both Houses shall be determined by Yeas and Nays, and the Names of the Persons voting for and against the Bill shall be entered on the Journal of each House respectively. If any Bill shall not be returned by the President within ten Days (Sundays excepted) after it shall have been presented to him, the Same shall be a Law, in like Manner as if he had signed it, unless the Congress by their Adjournment prevent its Return, in which Case it shall not be a Law.

Every Order, Resolution, or Vote to which the Concurrence of the Senate and House of Representatives may be necessary (except on a question of Adjournment) shall be presented to the President of the United States; and before the Same shall take Effect, shall be approved by him, or being disapproved by him, shall be repassed by two thirds of the Senate and House of Representatives, according to the Rules and Limitations prescribed in the Case of a Bill.

Section 8

The Congress shall have Power To lay and collect Taxes, Duties, Imposts and Excises, to pay the Debts and provide for the common Defence and general Welfare of the United States; but all Duties, Imposts and Excises shall be uniform throughout the United States;

✓ To borrow money on the credit of the United States;

✓ To regulate Commerce with foreign Nations, and among the several States, and with the Indian Tribes;

✓ To establish an uniform Rule of Naturalization, and uniform Laws on the subject of Bankruptcies throughout the United States;

✓ To coin Money, regulate the Value thereof, and of foreign Coin, and fix the Standard of Weights and Measures;

✓ To provide for the Punishment of counterfeiting the Securities and current Coin of the United States;

✓ To establish Post Offices and Post Roads;

✓ To promote the Progress of Science and useful Arts, by securing for limited Times to Authors and Inventors the exclusive Right to their respective Writings and Discoveries;

- ✓ To constitute Tribunals inferior to the supreme Court;

- ✓ To define and punish Piracies and Felonies committed on the high Seas, and Offenses against the Law of Nations;

- ✓ To declare War, grant Letters of Marque and Reprisal, and make Rules concerning Captures on Land and Water;

- ✓ To raise and support Armies, but no Appropriation of Money to that Use shall be for a longer Term than two Years;

- ✓ To provide and maintain a Navy;

- ✓ To make Rules for the Government and Regulation of the land and naval Forces;

- ✓ To provide for calling forth the Militia to execute the Laws of the Union, suppress Insurrections and repel Invasions;

- ✓ To provide for organizing, arming, and disciplining the Militia, and for governing such Part of them as may be employed in the Service of the United States, reserving to the States respectively, the Appointment of the Officers, and the Authority of training the Militia according to the discipline prescribed by Congress;

- ✓ To exercise exclusive Legislation in all Cases whatsoever, over such District (not exceeding ten Miles square) as may, by Cession of particular States, and the acceptance of Congress, become the Seat of the Government of the United States, and to exercise like Authority over all Places purchased by the Consent of the Legislature of the State in which the Same shall be, for the Erection of Forts, Magazines, Arsenals, dock-Yards, and other needful Buildings; And

- ✓ To make all Laws which shall be necessary and proper for carrying into Execution the foregoing Powers, and all other

Powers vested by this Constitution in the Government of the United States, or in any Department or Officer thereof.

Section 9

The Migration or Importation of such Persons as any of the States now existing shall think proper to admit, shall not be prohibited by the Congress prior to the Year one thousand eight hundred and eight, but a tax or duty may be imposed on such Importation, not exceeding ten dollars for each Person.

The privilege of the Writ of Habeas Corpus shall not be suspended, unless when in Cases of Rebellion or Invasion the public Safety may require it.

No Bill of Attainder or ex post facto Law shall be passed.

No capitation, or other direct, Tax shall be laid, unless in Proportion to the Census or Enumeration herein before directed to be taken.

No Tax or Duty shall be laid on Articles exported from any State.

No Preference shall be given by any Regulation of Commerce or Revenue to the Ports of one State over those of another: nor shall Vessels bound to, or from, one State, be obliged to enter, clear, or pay Duties in another.

No Money shall be drawn from the Treasury, but in Consequence of Appropriations made by Law; and a regular Statement and Account of the Receipts and Expenditures of all public Money shall be published from time to time.

No Title of Nobility shall be granted by the United States: And no Person holding any Office of Profit or Trust under them, shall, without the Consent of the Congress, accept of any present, Emolument, Office, or Title, of any kind whatever, from any King, Prince or foreign State.

Section 10

No State shall enter into any Treaty, Alliance, or Confederation; grant Letters of Marque and Reprisal; coin Money; emit Bills of Credit; make any Thing but gold and silver Coin a Tender in Payment of Debts; pass any Bill of Attainder, ex post facto Law, or Law impairing the Obligation of Contracts, or grant any Title of Nobility.

No State shall, without the Consent of the Congress, lay any Imposts or Duties on Imports or Exports, except what may be absolutely necessary for executing its inspection Laws: and the net Produce of all Duties and Imposts, laid by any State on Imports or Exports, shall be for the Use of the Treasury of the United States; and all such Laws shall be subject to the Revision and Control of the Congress.

No State shall, without the Consent of Congress, lay any duty of Tonnage, keep Troops, or Ships of War in time of Peace, enter into any Agreement or Compact with another State, or with a foreign Power, or engage in War, unless actually invaded, or in such imminent Danger as will not admit of delay.

ARTICLE II

Section 1

The executive Power shall be vested in a President of the United States of America. He shall hold his Office during the Term of four Years, and, together with the Vice-President chosen for the same Term, be elected, as follows:

Each State shall appoint, in such Manner as the Legislature thereof may direct, a Number of Electors, equal to the whole Number of Senators and Representatives to which the State may be entitled in the Congress: but no Senator or Representative, or Person holding an Office of Trust or Profit under the United States, shall be appointed an Elector.

The Electors shall meet in their respective States, and vote by Ballot for two persons, of whom one at least shall not lie an Inhabitant of the same State with themselves. And they shall make a List of all the Persons voted for, and of the Number of Votes for each; which List they shall sign and certify, and transmit sealed to the Seat of the Government of the United States, directed to the President of the Senate. The President of the Senate shall, in the Presence of the Senate and House of Representatives, open all the Certificates, and the Votes shall then be counted. The Person having the greatest Number of Votes shall be the President, if such Number be a Majority of the whole Number of Electors appointed; and if there be more than one who have such Majority, and have an equal Number of Votes, then the House of Representatives shall immediately choose by Ballot one of them for President; and if no Person have a Majority, then from the five highest on the List the said House shall in like Manner choose the President. But in choosing the President, the Votes shall be taken by States, the Representation from each State having one Vote; a quorum for this Purpose shall consist of a Member or Members from two-thirds of the States, and a Majority of all the States shall be necessary to a Choice. In every Case, after the Choice of the President, the Person having the greatest Number of Votes of the Electors shall be the Vice President. But if there should remain two or more who have equal Votes, the Senate shall choose from them by Ballot the Vice-President.

The Congress may determine the Time of choosing the Electors, and the Day on which they shall give their Votes; which Day shall be the same throughout the United States.

No person except a natural born Citizen, or a Citizen of the United States, at the time of the Adoption of this Constitution, shall be eligible to the Office of President; neither shall any Person be eligible to that Office who shall not have attained to the Age of thirty-five Years, and been fourteen Years a Resident within the United States.

In Case of the Removal of the President from Office, or of his Death, Resignation, or Inability to discharge the Powers and Duties of the said Office, the same shall devolve on the Vice President, and the Congress may by Law provide for the Case of Removal, Death, Resignation or Inability, both of the President and Vice President, declaring what Officer shall then act as President, and such Officer shall act accordingly, until the Disability be removed, or a President shall be elected.

The President shall, at stated Times, receive for his Services, a Compensation, which shall neither be increased nor diminished during the Period for which he shall have been elected, and he shall not receive within that Period any other Emolument from the United States, or any of them.

Before he enter on the Execution of his Office, he shall take the following Oath or Affirmation:

"I do solemnly swear (or affirm) *that I will faithfully execute the Office of President of the United States, and will to the best of my Ability, preserve, protect and defend the Constitution of the United States."*

Section 2

The President shall be Commander in Chief of the Army and Navy of the United States, and of the Militia of the several States, when called into the actual Service of the United States; he may require the Opinion, in writing, of the principal Officer in each of the executive Departments, upon any subject relating to the Duties of their respective Offices, and he shall have Power to Grant Reprieves and Pardons for Offenses against the United States, except in Cases of Impeachment.

He shall have Power, by and with the Advice and Consent of the Senate, to make Treaties, provided two thirds of the Senators present concur; and he shall nominate, and by and with the Advice and Consent of the Senate, shall appoint Ambassadors, other public Ministers and Consuls, Judges of the supreme Court, and all other Officers of the United States, whose Appointments are not herein otherwise provided for, and which shall be established by Law: but the Congress may by Law vest the Appointment of such inferior Officers, as they think proper, in the President alone, in the Courts of Law, or in the Heads of Departments.

The President shall have Power to fill up all Vacancies that may happen during the Recess of the Senate, by granting Commissions which shall expire at the End of their next Session.

Section 3

He shall from time to time give to the Congress Information of the State of the Union, and recommend to their Consideration such Measures as he shall judge necessary and expedient; he may, on extraordinary Occasions, convene both Houses, or either of them, and in Case of Disagreement between them, with Respect to the Time of Adjournment, he may adjourn them to such Time as he shall think proper; he shall receive Ambassadors and other public Ministers; he shall take Care that the Laws be faithfully executed, and shall Commission all the Officers of the United States.

Section 4

The President, Vice President and all civil Officers of the United States, shall be removed from Office on Impeachment for, and Conviction of, Treason, Bribery, or other high Crimes and Misdemeanors.

ARTICLE III

Section 1

The judicial Power of the United States, shall be vested in one supreme Court, and in such inferior Courts as the Congress may from time to time ordain and establish. The Judges, both of the supreme and inferior Courts, shall hold their Offices during good Behavior, and shall, at stated Times, receive for their Services a Compensation which shall not be diminished during their Continuance in Office.

Section 2

The judicial Power shall extend to all Cases, in Law and Equity, arising under this Constitution, the Laws of the United States, and Treaties made, or which shall be made, under their Authority; to all Cases affecting Ambassadors, other public Ministers and Consuls; to all Cases of admiralty and maritime Jurisdiction; to Controversies to which the United States shall be a Party; to Controversies between two or more States; between a State and Citizens of another State; between Citizens of different States; between Citizens of the same State claiming Lands under Grants of different States, and between a State, or the Citizens thereof, and foreign States, Citizens or Subjects.

In all Cases affecting Ambassadors, other public Ministers and Consuls, and those in which a State shall be Party, the supreme Court shall have original Jurisdiction. In all the other Cases before mentioned, the supreme Court shall have appellate Jurisdiction, both as to Law and Fact, with such Exceptions, and under such Regulations as the Congress shall make.

The Trial of all Crimes, except in Cases of Impeachment, shall be by Jury; and such Trial shall be held in the State where the said Crimes shall have been committed; but when not committed within any State, the Trial shall be at such Place or Places as the Congress may by Law have directed.

Section 3

Treason against the United States, shall consist only in levying War against them, or in adhering to their Enemies, giving them Aid and Comfort. No Person shall be convicted of Treason unless on the Testimony of two Witnesses to the same overt Act, or on Confession in open Court.

The Congress shall have power to declare the Punishment of Treason, but no Attainder of Treason shall work Corruption of Blood, or Forfeiture except during the Life of the Person attainted.

ARTICLE IV

Section 1

Full Faith and Credit shall be given in each State to the public Acts, Records, and judicial Proceedings of every other State. And the Congress may by general Laws prescribe the Manner in which such Acts, Records and Proceedings shall be proved, and the Effect thereof.

Section 2

The Citizens of each State shall be entitled to all Privileges and Immunities of Citizens in the several States.

A Person charged in any State with Treason, Felony, or other Crime, who shall flee from Justice, and be found in another State, shall on demand of the executive Authority of the State from which he fled, be delivered up, to be removed to the State having Jurisdiction of the Crime.

No Person held to Service or Labour in one State, under the Laws thereof, escaping into another, shall, in Consequence of any Law or Regulation therein, be discharged from such Service or Labour, But shall be delivered up on Claim of the Party to whom such Service or Labour may be due.

Section 3

New States may be admitted by the Congress into this Union; but no new States shall be formed or erected within the Jurisdiction of any other State; nor any State be formed by the Junction of two or more States, or parts of States, without the Consent of the Legislatures of the States concerned as well as of the Congress.

The Congress shall have Power to dispose of and make all needful Rules and Regulations respecting the Territory or other Property belonging to the United States; and nothing in this Constitution shall be so construed as to Prejudice any Claims of the United States, or of any particular State.

Section 4

The United States shall guarantee to every State in this Union a Republican Form of Government, and shall protect each of them against Invasion; and on Application of the Legislature, or of the Executive (when the Legislature cannot be convened) against domestic Violence.

ARTICLE V

The Congress, whenever two thirds of both Houses shall deem it necessary, shall propose Amendments to this Constitution, or, on the Application of the Legislatures of two thirds of the several States, shall call a Convention for proposing Amendments, which, in either Case, shall be valid to all Intents and Purposes, as part of this Constitution, when ratified by the Legislatures of three fourths of the several States, or by Conventions in three fourths thereof, as the one or the other Mode of Ratification may be proposed by the Congress; Provided that no Amendment which may be made prior to the Year One thousand eight hundred and eight shall in any Manner affect the first and fourth Clauses in the Ninth Section of the first Article; and that no State, without its Consent, shall be deprived of its equal Suffrage in the Senate.

ARTICLE VI

All Debts contracted and Engagements entered into, before the Adoption of this Constitution, shall be as valid against the United States under this Constitution, as under the Confederation.

This Constitution, and the Laws of the United States which shall be made in Pursuance thereof; and all Treaties made, or which shall be made, under the Authority of the United States, shall be the supreme Law of the Land; and the Judges in every State shall be bound thereby, any Thing in the Constitution or Laws of any State to the Contrary notwithstanding.

The Senators and Representatives before mentioned, and the Members of the several State Legislatures, and all executive and judicial Officers, both of the United States and of the several States, shall be bound by Oath or Affirmation, to support this Constitution; but no religious Test shall ever be required as a Qualification to any Office or public Trust under the United States.

ARTICLE VII

The Ratification of the Conventions of nine States, shall be sufficient for the Establishment of this Constitution between the States so ratifying the Same.

Done in Convention by the Unanimous Consent of the States present the Seventeenth Day of September in the Year of our Lord one thousand seven hundred and Eighty seven and of the Independence of the United States of America the Twelfth. In Witness whereof we have hereunto subscribed our Names.

PRESIDENT AND DEPUTY FROM VIRGINIA
George Washington

NEW HAMPSHIRE
John Langdon • Nicholas Gilman

MASSACHUSETTS
Nathaniel Gorham • Rufus King

CONNECTICUT
William Samuel Johnson • Roger Sherman

NEW YORK
Alexander Hamilton

NEW JERSEY
William Livingston • David Brearley • William Paterson • Jonathan Dayton

PENNSYLVANIA
*Benjamin Franklin • Thomas Mifflin • Robert Morris • George Clymer
• Thomas Fitzsimons • Jared Ingersoll • James Wilson • Gouverneur Morris*

DELAWARE
*George Read • Gunning Bedford Jr. • John Dickinson • Richard Bassett
• Jacob Broom*

MARYLAND
James McHenry • Daniel of St Thomas Jenifer • Daniel Carroll

VIRGINIA
John Blair • James Madison Jr.

NORTH CAROLINA
William Blount • Richard Dobbs Spaight • Hugh Williamson

SOUTH CAROLINA
*John Rutledge • Charles Cotesworth Pinckney • Charles Pinckney
• Pierce Butler*

GEORGIA
William Few • Abraham Baldwin

ATTEST: *William Jackson, Secretary*

Amendment 1

Congress shall make no law respecting an establishment of religion, or prohibiting the free exercise thereof; or abridging the freedom of speech, or of the press; or the right of the people peaceably to assemble, and to petition the Government for a redress of grievances.

Amendment 2

A well regulated Militia, being necessary to the security of a free State, the right of the people to keep and bear Arms, shall not be infringed.

Amendment 3

No Soldier shall, in time of peace be quartered in any house, without the consent of the Owner, nor in time of war, but in a manner to be prescribed by law.

Amendment 4

The right of the people to be secure in their persons, houses, papers, and effects, against unreasonable searches and seizures, shall not be violated, and no Warrants shall issue, but upon probable cause, supported by Oath or affirmation, and particularly describing the place to be searched, and the persons or things to be seized.

Amendment 5

No person shall be held to answer for a capital, or otherwise infamous crime, unless on a presentment or indictment of a Grand Jury, except in cases arising in the land or naval forces, or in the Militia, when in actual service in time of War or public danger; nor shall any person be subject for the same offense to be twice put in jeopardy of life or limb; nor shall be compelled in any criminal case to be a witness against himself, nor be deprived of life, liberty, or property, without due process of law; nor shall private property be taken for public use, without just compensation.

Amendment 6

In all criminal prosecutions, the accused shall enjoy the right to a speedy and public trial, by an impartial jury of the State and district wherein the crime shall have been committed, which district shall have been previously ascertained by law, and to be informed of the nature and cause of the accusation; to be confronted with the witnesses against him; to have compulsory process for obtaining witnesses in his favor, and to have the Assistance of Counsel for his defense.

Amendment 7

In Suits at common law, where the value in controversy shall exceed twenty dollars, the right of trial by jury shall be preserved, and no fact tried by a jury, shall be otherwise reexamined in any Court of the United States, than according to the rules of the common law.

Amendment 8

Excessive bail shall not be required, nor excessive fines imposed, nor cruel and unusual punishments inflicted.

Amendment 9

The enumeration in the Constitution, of certain rights, shall not be construed to deny or disparage others retained by the people.

Amendment 10

The powers not delegated to the United States by the Constitution, nor prohibited by it to the States, are reserved to the States respectively, or to the people.

Amendment 11

The Judicial power of the United States shall not be construed to extend to any suit in law or equity, commenced or prosecuted against one of the United States by Citizens of another State, or by Citizens or Subjects of any Foreign State.

Amendment 12

The Electors shall meet in their respective states, and vote by ballot for President and Vice-President, one of whom, at least, shall not be an inhabitant of the same state with themselves; they shall name in their ballots the person voted for as President, and in distinct ballots the person voted for as Vice-President, and they shall make distinct lists of all persons voted for as President, and of all persons voted for as Vice-President and of the number of votes for each, which lists they shall sign and certify, and transmit sealed to the seat of the government of the United States, directed to the President of the Senate;

The President of the Senate shall, in the presence of the Senate and House of Representatives, open all the certificates and the votes shall then be counted;

The person having the greatest Number of votes for President, shall be the President, if such number be a majority of the whole number of Electors appointed; and if no person have such majority, then from the persons having the highest numbers not exceeding three on the list of those voted for as President, the House of Representatives shall choose immediately, by ballot, the President. But in choosing the President, the votes shall be taken by states, the representation from each state having one vote; a quorum for this purpose shall consist of a member or members from two-thirds of the states, and a majority of all the states shall be necessary to a choice. And if the House of Representatives shall not choose a President whenever the right of choice shall devolve upon them, before the fourth day of March next following, then the Vice-President shall act as President, as in the case of the death or other constitutional disability of the President.

The person having the greatest number of votes as Vice-President, shall be the Vice President, if such number be a majority of the whole number of Electors appointed, and if no person have a majority, then from the two highest numbers on the list, the Senate shall choose the Vice-President; a quorum for the purpose shall consist of two-thirds of the whole number of Senators, and a majority of the whole number shall be necessary to a choice. But no person constitutionally ineligible to the office of President shall be eligible to that of Vice-President of the United States.

Amendment 13

1. Neither slavery nor involuntary servitude, except as a punishment for crime whereof the party shall have been duly convicted, shall exist within the United States, or any place subject to their jurisdiction.

2. Congress shall have power to enforce this article by appropriate legislation.

Amendment 14

1. All persons born or naturalized in the United States, and subject to the jurisdiction thereof, are citizens of the United States and of the State wherein they reside. No State shall make or enforce any law which shall abridge the privileges or immunities of citizens of the United States; nor shall any State deprive any person of life, liberty, or property, without due process of law; nor deny to any person within its jurisdiction the equal protection of the laws.

2. Representatives shall be apportioned among the several States according to their respective numbers, counting the whole number of persons in each State, excluding Indians not taxed. But when the right to vote at any election for the choice of electors for President and Vice-President of the United States, Representatives in Congress, the Executive and Judicial officers of a State, or the members of the Legislature thereof, is denied to any of the male inhabitants of such State, being twenty-one years of age, and citizens of the United States, or in any way

abridged, except for participation in rebellion, or other crime, the basis of representation therein shall be reduced in the proportion which the number of such male citizens shall bear to the whole number of male citizens twenty-one years of age in such State.

3. No person shall be a Senator or Representative in Congress, or elector of President and Vice-President, or hold any office, civil or military, under the United States, or under any State, who, having previously taken an oath, as a member of Congress, or as an officer of the United States, or as a member of any State legislature, or as an executive or judicial officer of any State, to support the Constitution of the United States, shall have engaged in insurrection or rebellion against the same, or given aid or comfort to the enemies thereof. But Congress may by a vote of two-thirds of each House, remove such disability.

4. The validity of the public debt of the United States, authorized by law, including debts incurred for payment of pensions and bounties for services in suppressing insurrection or rebellion, shall not be questioned. But neither the United States nor any State shall assume or pay any debt or obligation incurred in aid of insurrection or rebellion against the United States, or any claim for the loss or emancipation of any slave; but all such debts, obligations and claims shall be held illegal and void.

5. The Congress shall have power to enforce, by appropriate legislation, the provisions of this article.

Amendment 15

1. The right of citizens of the United States to vote shall not be denied or abridged by the United States or by any State on account of race, color, or previous condition of servitude.

2. The Congress shall have power to enforce this article by appropriate legislation.

Amendment 16

The Congress shall have power to lay and collect taxes on incomes, from whatever source derived, without apportionment among the several States, and without regard to any census or enumeration.

Amendment 17

The Senate of the United States shall be composed of two Senators from each State, elected by the people thereof, for six years; and each Senator shall have one vote. The electors in each State shall have the qualifications requisite for electors of the most numerous branch of the State legislatures.

When vacancies happen in the representation of any State in the Senate, the executive authority of such State shall issue writs of election to fill such vacancies: Provided, That the legislature of any State may empower the executive thereof to make temporary appointments until the people fill the vacancies by election as the legislature may direct.

This amendment shall not be so construed as to affect the election or term of any Senator chosen before it becomes valid as part of the Constitution.

Amendment 18

1. After one year from the ratification of this article the manufacture, sale, or transportation of intoxicating liquors within, the importation thereof into, or the exportation thereof from the United States and all territory subject to the jurisdiction thereof for beverage purposes is hereby prohibited.

2. The Congress and the several States shall have concurrent power to enforce this article by appropriate legislation.

3. This article shall be inoperative unless it shall have been ratified as an amendment to the Constitution by the legislatures of the

several States, as provided in the Constitution, within seven years from the date of the submission hereof to the States by the Congress.

Amendment 19

The right of citizens of the United States to vote shall not be denied or abridged by the United States or by any State on account of sex.

Congress shall have power to enforce this article by appropriate legislation.

Amendment 20

1. The terms of the President and Vice President shall end at noon on the 20th day of January, and the terms of Senators and Representatives at noon on the 3d day of January, of the years in which such terms would have ended if this article had not been ratified; and the terms of their successors shall then begin.

2. The Congress shall assemble at least once in every year, and such meeting shall begin at noon on the 3d day of January, unless they shall by law appoint a different day.

3. If, at the time fixed for the beginning of the term of the President, the President elect shall have died, the Vice President elect shall become President. If a President shall not have been chosen before the time fixed for the beginning of his term, or if the President elect shall have failed to qualify, then the Vice President elect shall act as President until a President shall have qualified; and the Congress may by law provide for the case wherein neither a President elect nor a Vice President elect shall have qualified, declaring who shall then act as President, or the manner in which one who is to act shall be selected, and such person shall act accordingly until a President or Vice President shall have qualified.

4. The Congress may by law provide for the case of the death of any of the persons from whom the House of Representatives may choose a President whenever the right of choice shall have devolved upon them, and for the case of the death of any of the persons from whom the Senate may choose a Vice President whenever the right of choice shall have devolved upon them.

5. Sections 1 and 2 shall take effect on the 15th day of October following the ratification of this article.

6. This article shall be inoperative unless it shall have been ratified as an amendment to the Constitution by the legislatures of three-fourths of the several States within seven years from the date of its submission.

Amendment 21

1. The eighteenth article of amendment to the Constitution of the United States is hereby repealed.

2. The transportation or importation into any State, Territory, or possession of the United States for delivery or use therein of intoxicating liquors, in violation of the laws thereof, is hereby prohibited.

3. The article shall be inoperative unless it shall have been ratified as an amendment to the Constitution by conventions in the several States, as provided in the Constitution, within seven years from the date of the submission hereof to the States by the Congress.

Amendment 22

1. No person shall be elected to the office of the President more than twice, and no person who has held the office of President, or acted as President, for more than two years of a term to which some other person was elected President shall be elected

to the office of the President more than once. But this Article shall not apply to any person holding the office of President, when this Article was proposed by the Congress, and shall not prevent any person who may be holding the office of President, or acting as President, during the term within which this Article becomes operative from holding the office of President or acting as President during the remainder of such term.

2. This article shall be inoperative unless it shall have been ratified as an amendment to the Constitution by the legislatures of three-fourths of the several States within seven years from the date of its submission to the States by the Congress.

Amendment 23

1. The District constituting the seat of Government of the United States shall appoint in such manner as the Congress may direct: A number of electors of President and Vice President equal to the whole number of Senators and Representatives in Congress to which the District would be entitled if it were a State, but in no event more than the least populous State; they shall be in addition to those appointed by the States, but they shall be considered, for the purposes of the election of President and Vice President, to be electors appointed by a State; and they shall meet in the District and perform such duties as provided by the twelfth article of amendment.

2. The Congress shall have power to enforce this article by appropriate legislation.

Amendment 24

1. The right of citizens of the United States to vote in any primary or other election for President or Vice President, for electors for President or Vice President, or for Senator or Representative in Congress, shall not be denied or abridged by the United States or any State by reason of failure to pay any poll tax or other tax.

2. The Congress shall have power to enforce this article by appropriate legislation.

Amendment 25

1. In case of the removal of the President from office or of his death or resignation, the Vice President shall become President.

2. Whenever there is a vacancy in the office of the Vice President, the President shall nominate a Vice President who shall take office upon confirmation by a majority vote of both Houses of Congress.

3. Whenever the President transmits to the President pro tempore of the Senate and the Speaker of the House of Representatives his written declaration that he is unable to discharge the powers and duties of his office, and until he transmits to them a written declaration to the contrary, such powers and duties shall be discharged by the Vice President as Acting President.

4. Whenever the Vice President and a majority of either the principal officers of the executive departments or of such other body as Congress may by law provide, transmit to the President pro tempore of the Senate and the Speaker of the House of Representatives their written declaration that the President is unable to discharge the powers and duties of his office, the Vice President shall immediately assume the powers and duties of the office as Acting President.

Thereafter, when the President transmits to the President pro tempore of the Senate and the Speaker of the House of Representatives his written declaration that no inability exists, he shall resume the powers and duties of his office unless the Vice President and a majority of either the principal officers of the executive department or of such other body as Congress may by law provide, transmit within four days to the President pro tempore of the Senate and the Speaker of the House of Representatives their written declaration that the President is unable to discharge the powers and duties of his office. Thereupon Congress shall decide the issue, assembling within forty eight hours for that purpose if not in session. If the Congress, within twenty one days after receipt of the latter written declaration, or, if Congress is not in session, within twenty one days after Congress is required to assemble, determines by two thirds vote of both Houses that the President is unable to discharge the powers and duties of his office, the Vice President shall continue to discharge the same as Acting President; otherwise, the President shall resume the powers and duties of his office.

Amendment 26

1. The right of citizens of the United States, who are eighteen years of age or older, to vote shall not be denied or abridged by the United States or by any State on account of age.

2. The Congress shall have power to enforce this article by appropriate legislation.

Amendment 27

No law, varying the compensation for the services of the Senators and Representatives, shall take effect, until an election of Representatives shall have intervened.

APPENDIX C: A DEFENSE OF THE BIBLE IN SCHOOLS

Dear Sir:

It is now several months since I promised to give you my reasons for preferring the Bible as a schoolbook to all other compositions. Before I state my arguments, I shall assume the five following propositions:

1. *That Christianity is the only true and perfect religion; and that in proportion as mankind adopt its principles and obey its precepts they will be wise and happy.*

2. *That a better knowledge of this religion is to be acquired by reading the Bible than in any other way.*

3. *That the Bible contains more knowledge necessary to man in his present state than any other book in the world.*

4. *That knowledge is most durable, and religious instruction most useful, when imparted in early life.*

5. *That the Bible, when not read in schools, is seldom read in any subsequent period of life.*

I. My arguments in favor of the use of the Bible as a school book are founded in the constitution of the human mind.

First of all, the memory is the first faculty which opens in the minds of children. Of how much consequence, then, must it be to impress it with the great truths of Christianity, before it is preoccupied with less interesting subjects.

Secondly, there is a peculiar aptitude in the minds of children for religious knowledge. I have constantly found them, in the first six or seven years of their lives, more inquisitive upon religious subjects than upon any others. And an ingenious instructor of youth has informed me that he has found young children more capable of receiving just ideas upon the most difficult tenets of religion than upon the most simple branches of human knowledge. It would be strange if it were otherwise, for God creates all His means to suit His ends. There must, of course, be a fitness between the human mind and the truths which are essential to its happiness.

Third, the influence of early impressions is very great upon subsequent life; and in a world where false prejudices do so much mischief, it would discover great weakness not to oppose them by such as are true. I grant that many men have rejected the impressions derived from the Bible; but how much soever these impressions may have been despised, I believe no man was ever early instructed in the truths of the Bible without having been made wiser or better by the early operation of these impressions upon his mind. Every just principle that is to be found in the writings of Voltaire is borrowed from the Bible; and the morality of Deists, which has been so much admired and praised where it has existed, has been, I believe, in most cases, the effect of habits produced by early instruction in the principles of Christianity.

Fourth, we are subject, by a general law of our natures, to what is called habit. Now, if the study of the Scriptures be necessary to our happiness at any time of our life, the sooner we begin to read them, the more we shall probably be attached to them; for it is peculiar to all the acts of habit, to become easy, strong, and agreeable by repetition.

Fifth, it is a law in our natures that we remember longest the knowledge we acquire by the greatest number of our senses. Now, a knowledge of the contents of the Bible is acquired in school by the aid of the eye and the ear, for children, after getting their lessons, read or repeat them to their instructors in an audible voice; of course, there is a presumption that this knowledge will be retained much longer than if it had been acquired in any other way.

Sixth, the interesting events and characters recorded and described in the Old and New Testaments are calculated, above all others, to seize upon all the faculties of the mind of children. The understanding, the memory, the imagination, the passions, and the moral powers are all occasionally addressed by the various incidents which are contained in those divine books, insomuch that not to be delighted with them is to be devoid of every principle of pleasure that exists in a sound mind.

Seventh, there is in man a native preference of truth to fiction. Lord Shaftesbury says that *"truth is so congenial to our mind that we love even the shadow of it"*; and Horace, in his rules for composing an epic poem, established the same law in our natures by advising that *"fictions in poetry should resemble truth."* Now, the Bible contains more truth than any other book in the world; so true is the testimony that it bears of God in His works of creation, providence, and redemption that it is called truth itself, by way of preeminence above other things that are acknowledged to be true. How forcibly are we struck with the evidence of truth in the history of the Jews, above what we discover in the history of other nations. Where do we find a hero or an historian record his own faults or vices except in the Old Testament? Indeed, my friend, from some accounts which I have read of the American Revolution, I begin to grown skeptical to all history except that which is contained in the Bible. Now, if this book be known to contain nothing but what is materially true, the mind will naturally acquire a love for it from this circumstance; and from this affection for the truths of the Bible, it will acquire a discernment of truth in other books, and a preference of it in all the transactions of life.

Last of all, there is wonderful property in the memory which enables it in old age to recover the knowledge acquired in early life after it had been apparently forgotten for forty or fifty years. Of how much consequence, then, must it be to fill the mind with that species of knowledge in childhood and youth which, when recalled in the decline of life, will support the soul under the infirmities of age and smooth the avenues of approaching death. The Bible is the only book which is capable of affording this support to old age; and it is for this reason that we find it resorted to with so much diligence and pleasure by such old people as have read it in early life. I can recollect many instances of this kind in persons who discovered no special attachment to the Bible in the meridian of their days, who have, notwithstanding, spent the evening of life in reading no other book. The late Sir John Pringle, physician to the queen of Great Britain, after passing a long life in camps and at court, closed it by studying the Scriptures. So anxious was he to increase his knowledge in them that he wrote to Dr. Michaelis, a learned professor of divinity in Germany, for an explanation of a difficult text of Scripture a short time before his death.

II. **MY SECOND ARGUMENT IN FAVOR OF THE USE OF THE BIBLE IN SCHOOLS IS FOUNDED UPON AN IMPLIED COMMAND OF GOD AND UPON THE PRACTICE OF SEVERAL OF THE WISEST NATIONS OF THE WORLD.**

In the sixth chapter of Deuteronomy, we find the following words, which are directly to my purpose: *"And thou shalt love the Lord thy God with all thine heart, and with all thy soul, and with all thy might. And these words, which I command thee this day, shall be in thine heart: And thou shalt teach them diligently unto thy children, and shalt talk of them when thou sittest in thine house, and when thou walkest by the way, and when thou liest down, and when thou risest up."*

It appears, moreover, from the history of the Jews, that they flourished as a nation in proportion as they honored and read the books of Moses, which contained the only revelation that God had made to the world. The law was not only neglected, but lost, during the general profligacy of manner which accompanied the long and wicked reign of Manasseh. But the discovery of it amid the rubbish of the temple by Josiah and its subsequent general use were followed by a return of national virtue and prosperity. We read further of the wonderful effects which the reading of the law by Ezra, after his return from his captivity in Babylon, had upon the Jews. They showed the sincerity of their repentance by their general reformation.

The learning of the Jews, for many years, consisted in a knowledge of the Scriptures. These were the textbooks of all the instruction that was given in the schools of their Prophets. It was by means of this general knowledge of their law that those Jews who wandered from Judea into other countries carried with them and propagated certain ideas of the true God among all the civilized nations upon the face of the earth. And it was from the attachment they retained to the Old Testament that they procured a translation of it into the Greek language, after they had lost the Hebrew tongue by their long absence from their native country. The utility of this translation, commonly called the Septuagint, in facilitating the progress of the Gospel is well known to all who are acquainted with the history of the first age of the Christian church.

But the benefits of an early and general acquaintance with the Bible were not confined to the Jewish nation; they have appeared in many countries in Europe since the Reformation. The industry and habits of order which distinguish many of the German nations are derived from their early instruction in the principles of Christianity by means of the Bible. In Scotland and in parts of New England, where the Bible has been long used as a schoolbook, the inhabitants are among the most enlightened in religions and science, the most strict in morals, and the most intelligent in human affairs of any people whose history has come to my knowledge upon the surface of the globe.

I wish to be excused from repeating here that if the Bible did not convey a single direction for the attainment of future happiness, it should be read in our schools in preference to all other books from its containing the greatest portion of that kind of knowledge which is calculated to produce private and public temporal happiness.

We err, not only in human affairs but in religion likewise, only because we do not *"know the Scriptures"* and obey their instructions. Immense truths, I believe, are concealed in them. The time, I have no doubt, will come when posterity will view and pity our ignorance of these truths as much as we do the ignorance sometimes manifested by the disciples of our Saviour, who knew nothing of the meaning of those plain passages in the Old Testament which were daily fulfilling before their eyes.

But further, we err, not only in religion but in philosophy likewise, because we *"do not know or believe the Scriptures."* The sciences have been compared to a circle, of which religion composes a part. To understand any one of them perfectly, it is necessary to have some knowledge of them all. Bacon, Boyle, and Newton included the Scriptures in the inquiries to which their universal geniuses disposed them, and their philosophy was aided by their knowledge in them. A striking agreement has been lately discovered between the history of certain events recorded in the Bible and some of the operations and productions of nature, particularly those which are related in Whitehurst's observation on the deluge, in Smith's account of the origin of the variety of color in the human species, and in Bruce's travels. It remains yet to be shown how many other events related in the Bible accord with some late important discoveries in the principles of medicine. The events and the principles alluded to mutually establish the truth of each other.

I know it is said that the familiar use of the Bible in our schools has a tendency to lessen a due reverence for it. But this objection, by proving too much, proves nothing. If familiarity lessens respect for divine things, then all those precepts of our religion which enjoin the daily or weekly worship of the Deity are improper. The Bible was not intended to represent a Jewish ark; and it is an anti-Christian idea to suppose that it can be profaned by being carried into a schoolhouse, or by being handled by children.

It is also said that a great part of the Old Testament is no way interesting to mankind under the present dispensation of the Gospel. But I deny that any of the books of the Old Testament are not interesting to mankind under the Gospel dispensation. Most of the characters, events, and ceremonies mentioned in them are personal, providential, or instituted types of the Messiah, all of which have been, or remain yet, to be fulfilled by Him. It is from an ignorance or neglect of these types that we have so many Deists in Christendom, for so irreftagably do they prove the truth of Christianity that I am sure a young man who had been regularly instructed in their meaning could never doubt afterwards of the truth of any of its principles. If any obscurity appears in these principles, it is only, to use the words of the poet, because they are dark with excessive brightness.

I know there is an objection among many people to teaching children doctrines of any kind, because they are liable to be controverted. But let us not be wiser than our Maker. If moral precepts alone could have reformed mankind, the mission of the Son of God into our world would have been unnecessary. He came to promulgate a system of doctrines, as well as a system of morals. The perfect morality of the Gospel rests upon a doctrine which, though often controverted, has never been refuted; I mean the vicarious life and death of the Son of God. This sublime and ineffable doctrine delivers us from the absurd hypothesis of modern philosophers concerning the foundation of moral obligation, and fixes it upon the eternal and self-moving principle of LOVE. It concentrates a whole system of ethics in a single text of Scripture: *"A new commandment I give unto you, that ye love one another, even as I have loved you."* By withholding the knowledge of this doctrine from children, we deprive ourselves of the best means of awakening moral sensibility in their minds. We do more; we furnish an argument for withholding from them a knowledge of the morality of the Gospel likewise; for this, in many instances, is as supernatural, and therefore as liable to be controverted, as any of the doctrines or miracles which are mentioned in the New Testament. The miraculous conception of the Saviour of the world by a virgin is not more opposed to the ordinary course of natural events, nor is the doctrine of the atonement more above human reason, than those moral precepts which command us to love our enemies or to die for our friends.

I cannot but suspect that the present fashionable practice of rejecting the Bible from our schools has originated with Deists. And they discover great ingenuity in this new mode of attacking Christianity. If they proceed in it, they will do more in half a century in extirpating our religion than Bolingbroke or Voltaire could have effected in a thousand years.

But passing by all other considerations, and contemplating merely the political institutions of the United States, I lament that we waste so much time and money in punishing crimes and take so little pains to prevent them. We profess to be republicans, and yet we neglect the only means of establishing and perpetuating our republican forms of government; that is, the universal education of our youth in the principles of Christianity by means of the Bible; for this divine book, above all others, favors that equality among mankind, that respect for just laws, and all those sober and frugal virtues which constitute the soul of republicanism.

Perhaps an apology may be necessary for my having presumed to write upon a subject so much above my ordinary studies. My excuse for it is that I thought a single mite from a member of a profession which has been frequently charged with skepticism in religion might attract the notice of persons who had often overlooked the more ample contributions, upon this subject, of gentlemen in other professions.

With great respect, I am, etc.

Benjamin Rush

BENJAMIN RUSH

SELECTED BIBLIOGRAPHY

Barton, David. *America: To Pray or Not to Pray?* Aledo, Tex.: WallBuilder Press., 1988.

Barton, David. *Celebrate Liberty!* Aledo, Tex.: WallBuilder Press., 2003.

Beller, James. *The Collegiate Baptist History Workbook.* St. Louis, Mo.: Prairie Fire Press, 2005.

Esposito, Johnny. *Temples of Darkness.* Long Beach, Calif.: Pacific Publications, 2001

Federer, William J. *America's God and Country Encyclopedia of Quotations.* St. Louis, Mo.: Amerisearch, Inc., 2000.

Gibbs, Jr., Dr. David and Jerry Newcombe. *One Nation Under God.* Seminole, Fla.: Christian Law Association, 2003.

Ham, Ken and Britt Beemer. *Already Gone.* Green Forest, Ark.: Master Books, 2010.

Harding, Dr. Chuck and Caleb Garraway, *America's Forgotten History: Our Biblical Constitution*, directed by Awake America and Evangelism Ministries. 25 min. A Prophet Productions film, 2009. DVD.

Headley, J. T. *The Chaplains and Clergy of the Revolution.* St. John, Ind.: Larry Harrison Publications, 2008.

Millard, Catherine. *The Rewriting of America's History.* Camp Hill, Pa.: Horizon House Publishers, 1991.

Spivey, Larkin. *Miracles of the American Revolution.* Chattanooga, Tenn.: God and Country Press, 2010.

ABOUT THE AUTHOR

Caleb Garraway was born into a Christian home on July 20, 1986 and was born into the family of God on November 9, 1994. At the age of 11, he was called to preach through the preaching of Dr. Jack Hyles at Pastor's School in Hammond, IN. While attending Oklahoma Baptist College, Caleb traveled on the men's singing group for four years and also worked at the Windsor Hills Baptist Church for two years.

God has burdened his heart with America—its young people and its lost souls. Through his evangelism ministry, he desires to stir up the hearts of American Christians to zealously reach the next generation before it is too late and to challenge young people to maintain the Cause for our Lord Jesus Christ. Many souls have been saved and many lives have been touched by his ministry. Caleb has written two other books, *Found Fully Faithful* and *Our Blessed Book*, challenging young people to know what they believe and why the Bible is God's Word.

Caleb and Katie were married on March 20, 2010. Pray for them as they travel—for Holy Spirit power, Holy Spirit passion, and lost souls to be rescued from the flames of Hell and added to the church.

CONTACT CALEB & KATIE GARRAWAY AT:

EVANGELISM MINISTRIES
$^c/_o$ WINDSOR HILLS BAPTIST CHURCH
5517 N.W. 23rd Street
Oklahoma City, OK 73127

www.thegarrawayfamily.com
calebandkatieg@gmail.com

917.412.0059